Thanks . . .

To Russell Lamb and John Winquist for leads on Nordic ski areas in Wyoming and contacts in Utah.

Great loads of appreciation to Joan Ziegler — intrepid adventurer, transportation superintendent and banzai skier — for moral support, tenacity, patience and for being a very good sport during the period of "grueling" research for this book.

To Steve Gibbons for time spent in the dark room.

And to the myriad of wonderful folks who live in these magnificent mountains.

CROSS COUNTRY SKI LODGES

Montana
Wyoming
Utah

Nancy Budrow and Jane Hartline

Sauvie Island Press

COVER DESIGN by Abigail Anstey

MAPS by Mark Gostnell

 Published by Sauvie Island Press, Rt. 1 Box 526, Portland, Oregon 97231.

Photographs by Nancy Budrow.

Library of Congress
Catalog Card No. 82-51030

Budrow, Nancy Smith & Hartline, Jane

Cross Country Ski Lodges: Montana, Wyoming, Utah.

Portland, OR: Sauvie Island Press

Contents

Montana

Northern Rockies

10 Izaak Walton Inn
14 Desert Mountain Guest Ranch
18 Star Meadows Ranch
22 Crystal Lakes Resort
26 Montana Sports Ranch
30 Holland Lake Lodge

Bitterroot Range

34 Lolo Hot Springs Resort
38 Sleeping Child Hot Springs
42 Lost Horse Nordic Village
46 Lost Trail Hot Springs

Big Hole Valley

50 Jackson Hot Springs
54 Elkhorn Hot Springs

Continental Divide

58 Fairmont Hot Springs
62 Sunshine Health Mines
66 Boulder Hot Springs

East of the Divide

70 7 Lazy P Ranch
74 Poor Farm Sportsman's Lodge
78 Lone Mountain Guest Ranch
82 Bridger Mountain Lodge
86 Chico Hot Springs
90 Burnt Leather Ranch
94 Hawley Mountain Guest Ranch

Wyoming

West of the Divide

100 Flagg Ranch
104 Triangle X Ranch
108 Western Motel
112 Camp Creek Inn
114 White Pine Lodge

East of the Divide

118 Rawhide Ranch
120 Pahaska Tepee
124 Old Faithful Snow Lodge
128 Wind River Ranch

Big Horn Mountains

132 Bear Lodge
134 Arrowhead Lodge
138 Meadowlark Lake Lodge

South Central

142 Esterbrook Lodge
144 Hotel Wolf
148 Medicine Bow Lodge

Utah

Wasatch Range

154 Chateau Apres
158 Piute Creek Outfitters
162 The Homestead
166 Silver Fork Lodge
170 Snowpine Lodge

Southern Utah

174 Mt. Holly Ski Resort
176 Bristlecone Hostel
180 Meadeau View Lodge
184 Ruby's Inn

188 Recommended References
189 Trail Information
194 Index

Introduction

Wrapped in blankets from eyebrows to toe nails, with only the pen hand emerging, the skier/writer made shivering efforts to work in a primitive log cabin that clear, cold winter night. She eventually gave up, stoked the open fire and disappeared into a sleeping bag. Despite two wool blankets layered on top of her Polarguard cocoon, she awakened several times during the night because of the frigid air. In the morning, postponing the dreaded event as long as possible, she finally slinked out of the mummy sack and rapidly pulled on wool cap, socks and jacket over long flannel nightgown and tights. From just inside the doorway she retrieved wood and axe off the porch, then hastily split kindling, laid the fire, lit a match... and relaxed.

The skiers went out that morning and each had a problem. One, using special green, discovered her hardest wax was too soft. The other found it necessary to stop repeatedly in the sun, remove boot and sock, and determine if the foot was still there. Upon their return to the cabin, the skiers learned the reason why their breakfast eggs were frozen, why their car wouldn't start and why a camera refused to function — the temperature had dropped to minus 30 degrees during the night.

The odyssey which preceded the writing of this book covered 7,300 miles, nine crossings of the Continental Divide, exploration of 46 lodges... and the above mini-drama. The awesome Rocky Mountains in winter.

When one considers the potential hazards on a trip of this nature and scope — avalanches, ski accidents, car wrecks, getting lost in a blizzard, frostbite, pneumonia, or even being run over by a bar stool ski racer — it's difficult to believe that the major calamity of the journey was a dog bite.

It was thrilling to discover a feature shared by Montana and Wyoming. That northerly region is home for a profusion of snow-land wildlife — within whispering distance to man. Vast herds of pronghorn antelope graze undisturbed alongside Wyoming freeways. Bison and wapiti elk know which turf is theirs and aren't bashful about utilizing it. And moose like to get in close to ranch barns and corrals.

The farther south one travels, into more populous territory, the less likely is the sighting of game. But in the Montana Rockies, and throughout most of Wyoming, you're almost guaranteed at least a glimpse of both white tail and mule deer, bighorn sheep, coyote, porcupine, bald eagles, rabbits, lots of birds and probably a mouse or two. And hundreds of elk, moose and bison.

Utah is primarily a downhill state because that's the way the territory tilts. The Wasatch Range is extremely steep — vertical is more specific — and loaded with Alpine resorts and lifts. The enviable and absurd proximity of the mountains to Salt Lake City makes for intensive and successful Alpine utilization. Tourers have, of necessity, learned xc downhill, telemarking, and "any which way you can" to negotiate the terrain.

All three states share the Rocky Mountains, have relatively comparable weather patterns, enjoy wondrous snow conditions and provide some of the most stunning winter scenery you can ever hope to see.

Montana

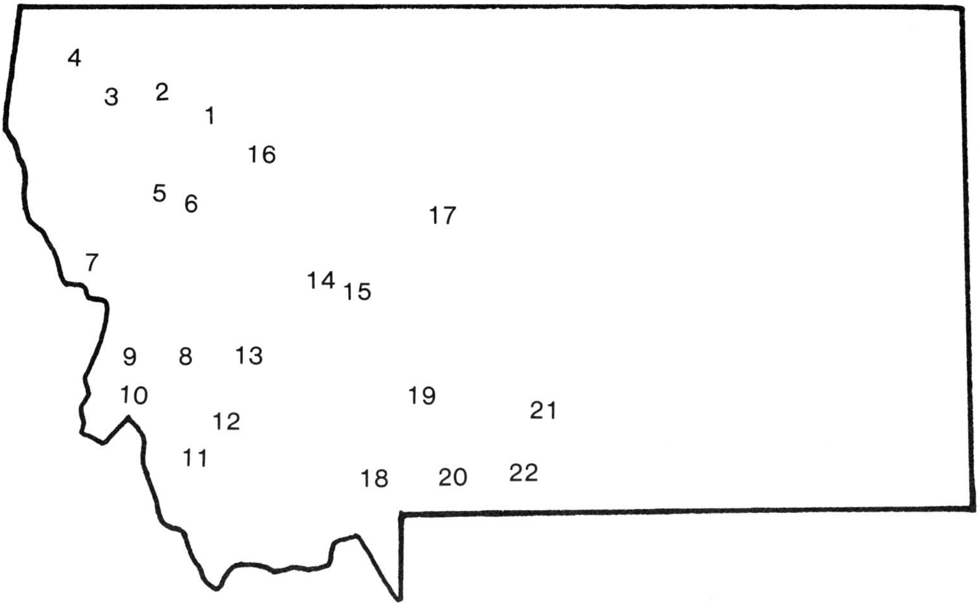

1 Izaak Walton Inn
2 Desert Mountain Guest Ranch
3 Star Meadows Ranch
4 Crystal Lakes Resort
5 Montana Sports Ranch
6 Holland Lake Lodge
7 Lolo Hot Springs Resort
8 Sleeping Child Hot Springs
9 Lost Horse Nordic Village
10 Lost Trail Hot Springs
11 Jackson Hot Springs
12 Elkhorn Hot Springs
13 Fairmont Hot Springs
14 Sunshine Health Mines
15 Boulder Hot Springs
16 7 Lazy P Ranch
17 Poor Farm Sportsman's Lodge
18 Lone Mountain Guest Ranch
19 Bridger Mountain Lodge
20 Chico Hot Springs
21 Burnt Leather Ranch
22 Hawley Mountain Guest Ranch

Izaak Walton Inn

Location
On U.S. 2 at Essex, Montana; 60 miles east of Kalispell; 30 miles east of West Glacier; 30 miles west of East Glacier.

Accommodations
26 lodge rooms, with or without private bath, each accommodating 1 to 3 persons. Total lodge capacity, 75. No kitchens. Rates start at $21 for 2.

Services
Laundromat, sauna, restaurant, bar, post office at lodge. Gas available 1 mile west (regular only). Groceries at Essex.

Trails and Snow Conditions
18 miles of set tracks adjacent to lodge. Almost unlimited ski touring in Flathead National Forest and in Glacier Park. Trail information available at Inn.

Ski Rentals and Lessons
Ski rentals and waxing room at lodge.

Reservations
Booking 6 months to a year ahead is advised for weekends; no problem during the week. Major credit cards. No pets.
Izaak Walton Inn
P.O. Box 675
Essex, MT 59916
Phone Essex #1 (Tell the operator to route the call via Great Falls.)

If Izaak Walton Inn is an example of Montana hospitality, you can believe there is good reason it's called the "Howdy" state.

Inn proprietors Sid and Millie Goodrich simply glow with goodwill and conviviality. Even if the lodge had no other amenities beyond the host and hostess (which is not the case), you would find yourself returning again and again like other guests, just to visit effervescent Millie and to delight in Sid's quintessentially arid sense of humor.

The Goodriches have filled their historic hotel with warmth and memorabilia. The Inn was built in 1939 by the Great Northern Railway for railroad personnel on duty in the area. (Workers from Burlington Northern, the rail line which resulted from a Great Northern merger, still stay at the Inn while clearing the tracks of snow.)

Top: Sid and Millie Goodrich offer guests a whole lot more than bed and bath. At Izaak Walton the visitor will find conviviality, hospitality and a twinkle in the eye. Below: The Essex inn was built by the railway in 1939.

The Inn houses collections of railroad lore including photographs of local train derailments and avalanches, dining room chandeliers crafted of green and red 1920-era kerosene lamp flag signals and an almost complete set of G.N. railroad tie nails. The nailheads were date-stamped every year from 1900 until the 1968 merger. Sid has at least one of each except 00 and 63.

A most unusual ceiling has replaced the old accoustical tile in the dining room. Millie designed the diagonal pattern of the knotty pine planking and Sid provided the trigonometry to the carpenters.

The downstairs "Flagstop" barroom is akin to a basement party room in the home of one's good friends. Sid sometimes holds forth behind the bar preparing his specialties – "Nordic Delight", hot chocolate and peppermint schnapps, and the "Nordic Dewaxer," a hot bourbon concoction. Rest your feet on the old track rail while sipping your toddy.

Top: Guests at Izaak Walton receive instructions on the way to the trails. Most trail heads are across the network of tracks from the Inn. Below: Although Amtrak doesn't stop at Essex, it does pass by several times a day.

There is something for everyone in the "rec room" — video disc movies, a piano, pool table, juke boxes, foosball and pin ball.

Outdoors at Essex, the name of the game is Cross Country Skiing. Sid machine-sets 18 miles of tracks heading from the hotel and there are miles of ungroomed trails in both adjacent Glacier Park and bordering Flathead National Forest. Try Autumn Creek Trail near the Continental Divide for a 6-mile back woods tour. Hitchhike or arrange a car shuttle back to your vehicle.

After a refreshing morning of skiing, treat yourself to a lunch of homemade thick corn chowder and hot-from-the-oven apple pie. At dinner you'll want to try the daily special. Inn chefs enjoy presenting meals from new recipes, and spend hours studying their cookbooks. Delicious results emerge from the kitchen.

The old Essex rail depot still stands, across the tracks from the hotel, but Amtrak doesn't stop there. To add another glorious dimension to your ski vacation, leave the car at home and have your group picked up at Belton, the West Glacier station, 30 miles westward. Both east and westbound passenger trains pass through there daily. Be sure to let railroad officaldom know your departure plans. Belton is only a flag stop and if you are to board your train after dark, the engineer can't see you patiently waiting.

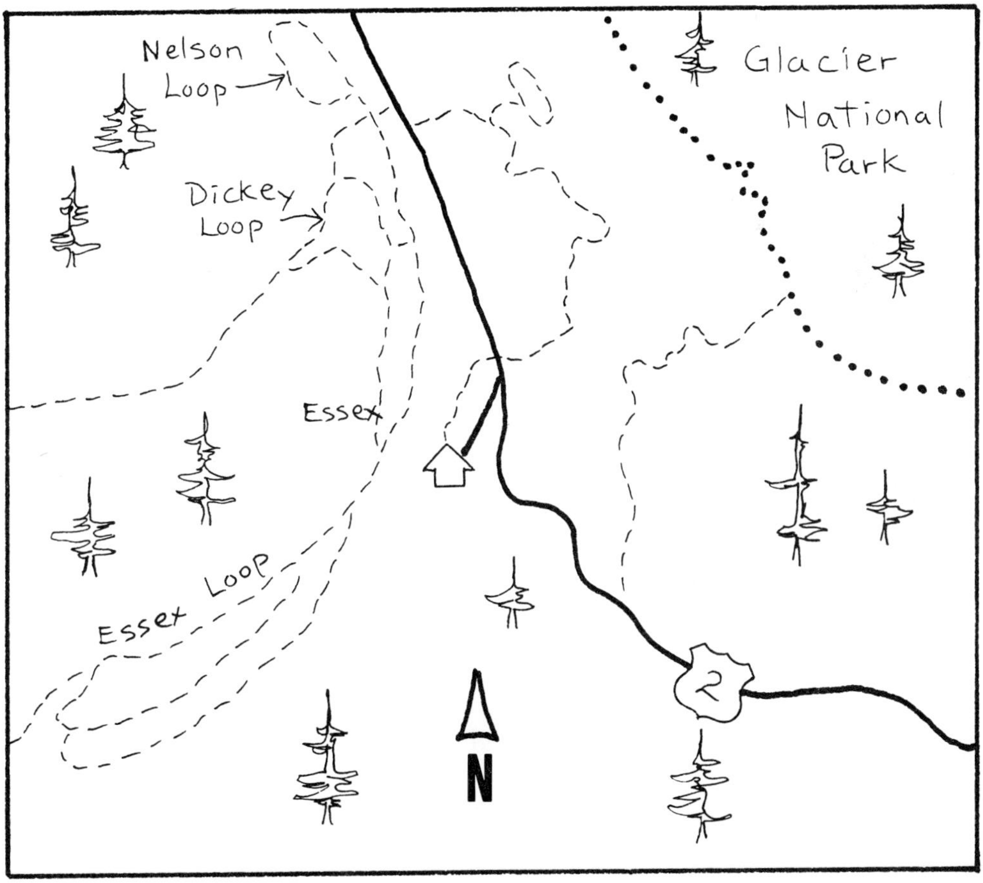

Desert Mountain Guest Ranch

Location
½ mile off U.S. 2, 4 miles west of West Glacier, Montana; 32 miles east of Whitefish; 27 miles northeast of Kalispell.

Accommodations
Cabins and "motel" type units with baths, some with fireplaces. No kitchens. Lodge rooms with or without private baths. Deluxe lodge suite features waterbed and private Jacuzzi. Resort capacity 50. Rates, starting at $28 for a single room, go to $45 for a suite accommodating 2 to 4. Lodging with all meals is $32 per person per day.

Services
Indoor pool, sauna, hot tub. Gas, groceries, restaurants within 4 miles at West Glacier, Coram or Hungry Horse.

Trails and Snow Conditions
40 miles of machine-made tracks, set daily, on 250-acre ranch. 2-3 feet of snow is typical level in this area.

Ski Rentals and Lessons
Complete ski rental services at ranch. Occasional ski clinics scheduled.

Reservations
Make winter reservations 2 weeks ahead. Make advance arrangement for pick-up at West Glacier Amtrak stop or at Kalispell, if arriving by air. MC, Visa. Pets are okay in rooms, but not on trails.

Desert Mountain Guest Ranch
P.O. Box 157
West Glacier, MT 59936
(406) 387-5610

Like to ride the train? Take along your friends and make a party of the journey? Plan a winter ski visit to Desert Mountain Guest Ranch near Glacier Park, and arrive by Amtrak undaunted.

West Glacier, a flag stop four miles down the highway from the ranch, is your rail destination. Ranch staff will pick you up there and tote you back to your lodgings at the base of 6,436-foot Desert Mountain.

Choose a private cabin or stay in a lovely modern lodge room, complete with carpeting, log-beamed ceiling and woodsy deck.

Ranch proprieters Alan and Helen Hay have been on-site managers for about 3½ years. Along with their efficient staff, they are doing a spectacular job of keeping guests happy — by running a well-maintained, clean operation; serving heaps of set-menu, family-style food and providing such amenities as 40 miles of machine-set tracks, a hot tub, sauna and indoor swimming pool.

Top: Lodging choices at Desert Mountain Guest Ranch include private cabins and simple to posh rooms in the main lodge. Below: An indoor swimming pool and sauna provide opportunities for relaxation after outdoor snow fun.

On a kitchen wall at the ranch hangs an artist's image of a winter ranch scene. The caption, by Emerson, seems to reflect the attitude of Desert Mountain hosts — "The ornaments of our house are the friends that frequent it."

The mountain resort has been a busy summer dude ranch for 45 years. And now, to keep things moving right along in the winter, the Hays attract xc skiers. They schedule a citizens' race in February and frequently book large groups into the lodge. A not-to-be-missed event, if one is in the area in late January, is Cabin Fever Days at nearby Martin City. Near the ranch, the Dew Drop Inn participates in the taking-leave-of-the-woods celebration by hosting an all you can eat chicken barbecue and providing live music and plenty of floor space for Saturday night stomping.

Don't miss the opportunity to tour into Glacier Park along "Going to the Sun Highway". Indians named the route thus because its mountainous climb seemed to lead directly into the sky. The road is plowed to the far end of Lake McDonald, so one has a head start to Avalanche Creek Campground or to other trails at

Top: Miles of set tracks at Desert Mountain follow level ranch pastureland and wooded hillside terrain. Below: Bar stool ski races are a featured competitive event at the January Cabin Fever Days, near the guest ranch.

either end of the lake. Stop at the Park headquarters, open year 'round, for maps and information.

If you find that there is no room at the lodge, try Glacier Highland at the west entrance to the Park. There is a motel, cafe, store and ski rental, and they're right across the highway from the Amtrak stop at West Glacier (Belton, in the RR time tables). Contact them at West Glacier, MT 59936; (406) 888-5427.

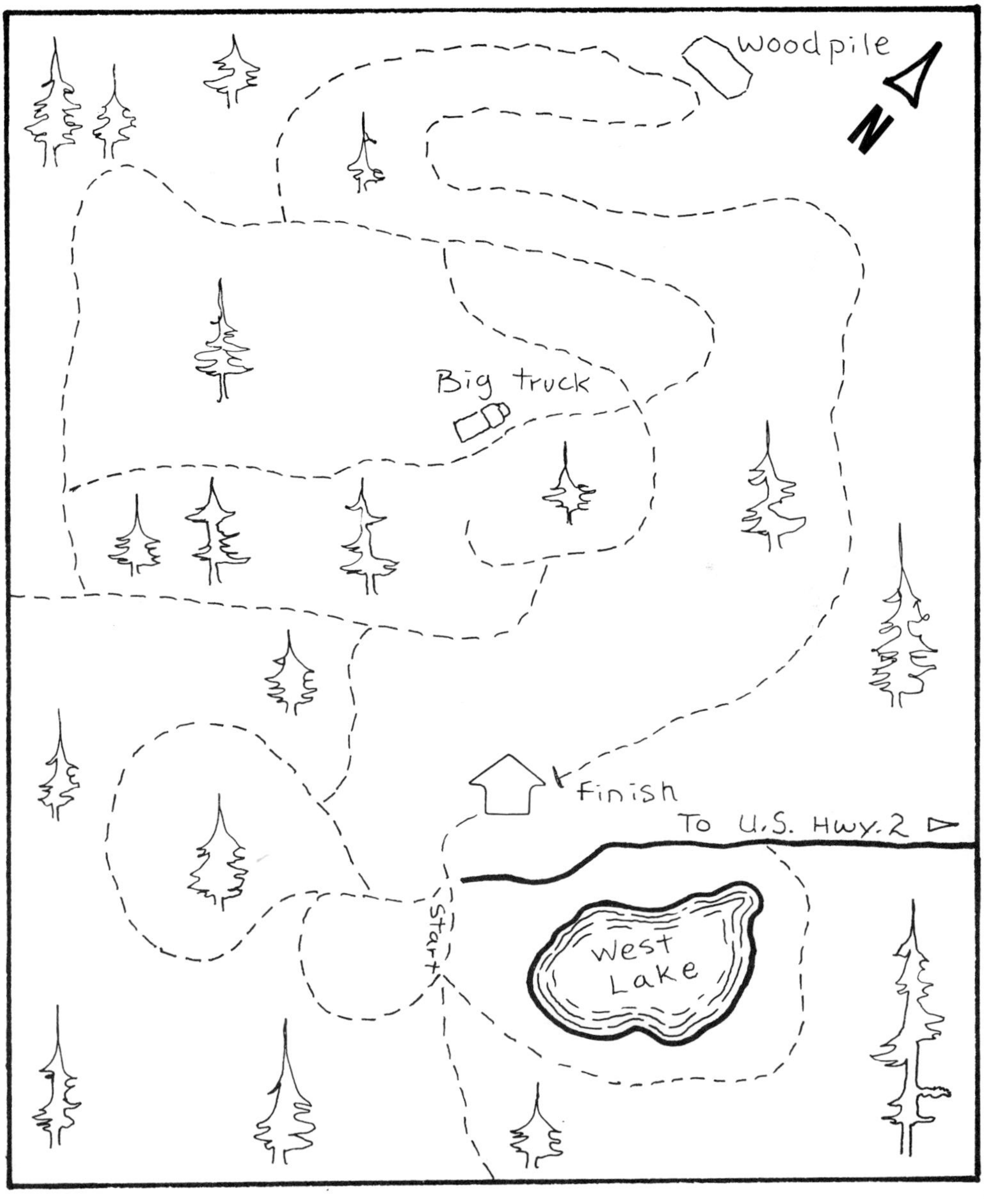

Star Meadows Ranch

Location
14 miles off U.S. 93; 24 miles northwest of Whitefish, Montana (turn west off 93 at Milepost 139).

Accommodations
Lodge rooms house 1-3 persons each, bath down the hall. 2 and 3 bedroom cabins have private baths. No kitchens. Resort capacity 47. Rates, starting at $30 per person, include all meals. Will reserve entire facilities to groups of 20 or more.

Services
All meals provided; bar, sauna. Other services at Whitefish.

Trails and Snow Conditions
25 kilometers of machine-packed and set tracks. Miles of groomed and ungroomed trails on forest service land. Usual snow depth, 4 feet. Trail day use fee $2; with lunch $6 (no charge to lodge guests).

Ski Rentals and Lessons
All rental, PSIA instruction levels and guide services available at ranch. Waxing and first aid room. Instruction also available at golf course in Whitefish.

Reservations
Weekdays, no problem. Reserve early for groups. No credit cards.
Star Meadows Ranch
Rt. 2
Whitefish, MT 59937
(406) 755-8230 (mobile unit)

At Star Meadows Ranch the aura says, "Come on in — make yourself at home." Resident proprietors Gail and Rick Towner are such relaxed folks that guests feel welcome to build a fire in one of the massive lodge fireplaces, lean back, put up their feet and anticipate the morrow's ski tour.

Bountiful meals are served family-style at long tables in the large, ground-level room overlooking the meadows. Food is like the hosts — wholesome and natural.

Third-story guest rooms are comfortable and very large. Many have a view of the meadows. Cabins are immediately adjacent to the lodge.

Rick and Gail arrived at the 27-horse, 2-mule summer dude ranch in 1977 and have been operating it year around ever since. Rich machine sets 25 kilometers of tracks on both meadow and wooded hillside terrain, on ranch property as well as on adjacent national forest land. This

Top: Gail and Rick Towner, manager/operators of Star Meadows Ranch, enjoy breaking bread with visitors. Lodging at the guest spread includes all meals. Below: Access to the ranch is via logging road, 24 miles from town.

is not your everyday, manicured trail experience. The trails are uncrowded and immediately depart the lodge area, taking you to vast meadows and forested hillsides. You get all the exhileration of a back woods ski trip with the ease of a beautifully packed snow route.

The "outback" flavor comes partly from the fact that the ranch is 24 miles from the nearest town and 14 miles off the highway on a logging road. Don't be deceived by these winter distances, however. Montana does an incredibly efficient job of plowing and maintaining roads and Star Meadows Ranch, though not served by mail or school bus, is extremely accessible without tire chains.

Originally a homestead plot, the 4,000-foot elevation ranch was named for the lowland it encompasses. The meadow drainage system consists of several arms which, from the air, resemble a star pattern.

Although the ranch environment is completely self-contained and everything a ski tourer could desire, there are some fun things to do in town. For skiing, the forest service signs trails and sets 25+ kilometers of track at Round Meadow – on the road to Star Meadows Ranch.

Lots of xc activity goes on in nearest-town Whitefish — the golf course is the site of well-maintained trails and many racing events throughout the season. For the bi-schusser, Big Mountain, just out of Whitefish, not only is big on downhilling, but now seeks to attract the skinny skier as well. A winter carnival is *the* event in Whitefish the first weekend of each February. Numerous citizens' ski

Skiers will find trail access from the door of the lodge at Star Meadows. Meticulously maintained set tracks lead for miles through vast meadows and across timbered hillsides.

races, the annual Cabin Fever Days in January plus multi-sport spring competitions provide entertainment for spectators as well as eager participants.

For eats in town, try Mister P's where a marvelous all-you-can-eat salad bar awaits at $2.50. Brothers Cafe is a good lunch choice and Hungry Hunky, at the south end of town, features a salad and beef pig-out on Friday and Saturday nights.

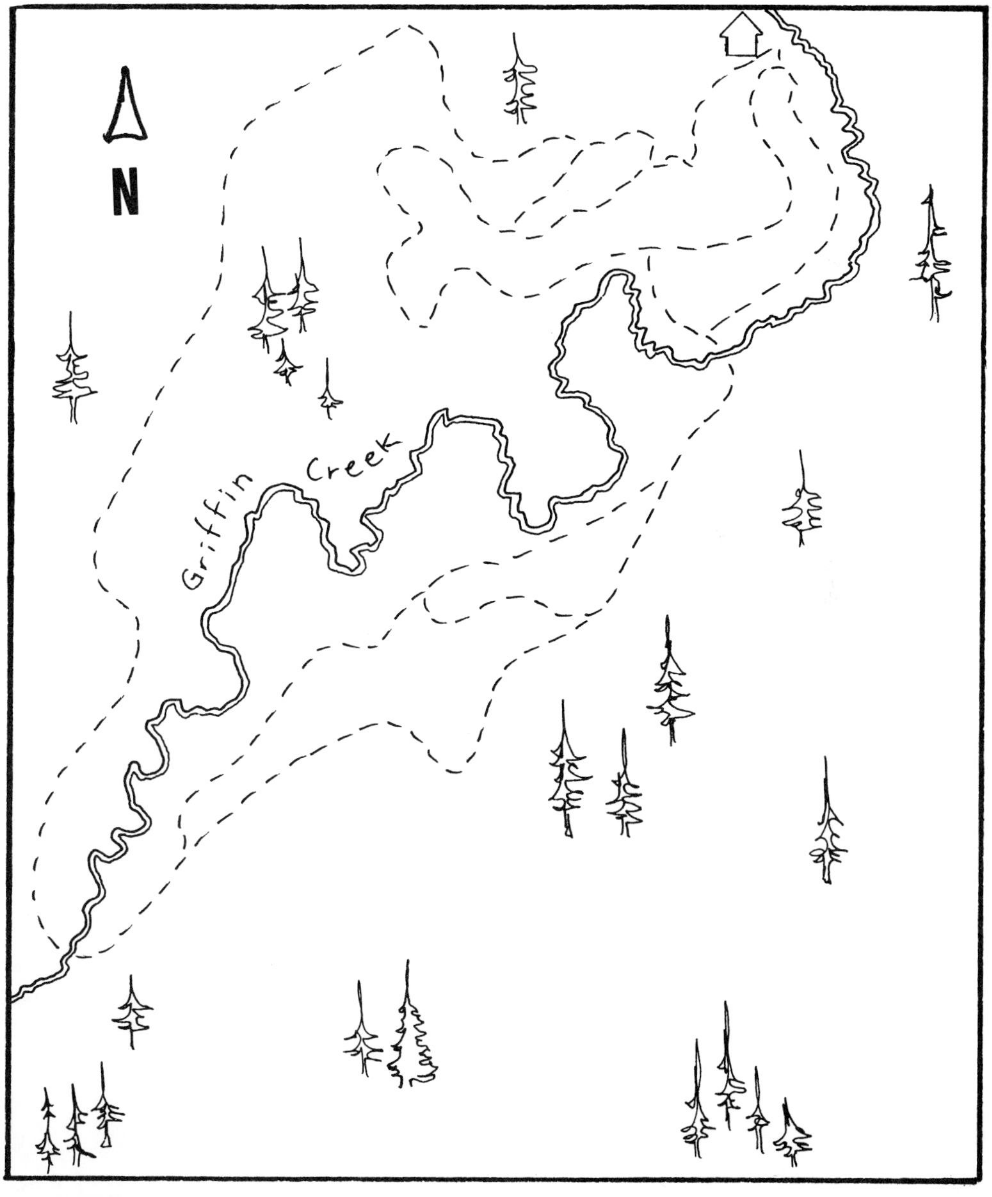

Crystal Lakes Resort

Location
1½ miles off U.S. 93, 17 miles south of Canadian border town Roosville. 45 miles north of Whitefish, Montana.

Accommodations
38 posh units sleep 2-8 people each. Some with fireplaces and/or kitchens. Kitchens are completely furnished. Total resort capacity 160. Rates from $14.50 to $35.00 per person per night.

Services
Restaurant, full-service bar, air strip, golf and apparel shop at resort. Groceries, gas and post office at nearby Fortine.

Trails and Snow Conditions
Up to 8 miles of machine-set tracks on premises. 18 inch snow and 25 degree temperature average. Wilderness trails in nearby Ten Lakes Scenic Area.

Ski Rentals and Lessons
Rental shop. Certified PSIA instruction for all ability levels; make arrangements in advance. Guide service for day tours or to overnight cabins available for advanced skiers.

Reservations
Major credit cards.
Crystal Lakes Resort
Fortine, MT 59918
(406) 882-4455

A destination golf resort in summer, Crystal Lakes is making an effort to attract winter visitors by machine-setting up to eight miles of tracks on the 520-acre premises; by offering xc ski lessons and guided tours; and by snow plowing the 5,000-foot airstrip adjacent to the lodge.

This resort has potential simply gushing out the bark of its pine trees, and management of the former working ranch advises that Crystal Lakes is "Montana's Best Kept Secret." The new owners, who took over four years ago, have made dramatic changes in the resort. But so far, the most obvious alterations are subdivision of the former working ranch into residential lots and the construction of condominiums. Thirty-eight of the privately-owned condos are available for rental.

Be advised that golf is the name of the game here (Arnold Palmer is designing the second nine holes). Although not much else but a few conferences appear to be scheduled for the winter, Nordic skiers don't seem to rank really high on the priority scale.

Above: Guest accommodations at Crystal Lakes Resort in northern Montana provide near-luxury and utmost comfort. Below: A summer golf area, the resort attracts winter tourers by setting a system of tracks on the property.

Weekend events for skiers include family and children's races as well as "sno-golf", a competition on skis, played with golf clubs and a racquetball. Many local attendees participate in these festivities.

For those who don't abide footprints of various sorts on their ski tracks, take note: at Crystal Lakes there is an abundance of deer spoor on the trails. It is reported that bald eagles, bear, elk, moose and whitetail deer regularly frequent the premises.

At 3,100-feet, the resort doesn't always have snow, but 18 inches is not considered unusual. Average temperature is 25 degrees.

Although live music is usually provided in the lounge on weekends, best to bring your own group for entertainment. Crystal Lakes is a quiet place in winter.

Modern facilities at Crystal Lakes Resort are augmented by an interesting and picturesque old back bar, typical of early-Montana prosperity. Spacious dining areas offer airy surroundings and a view of the grounds.

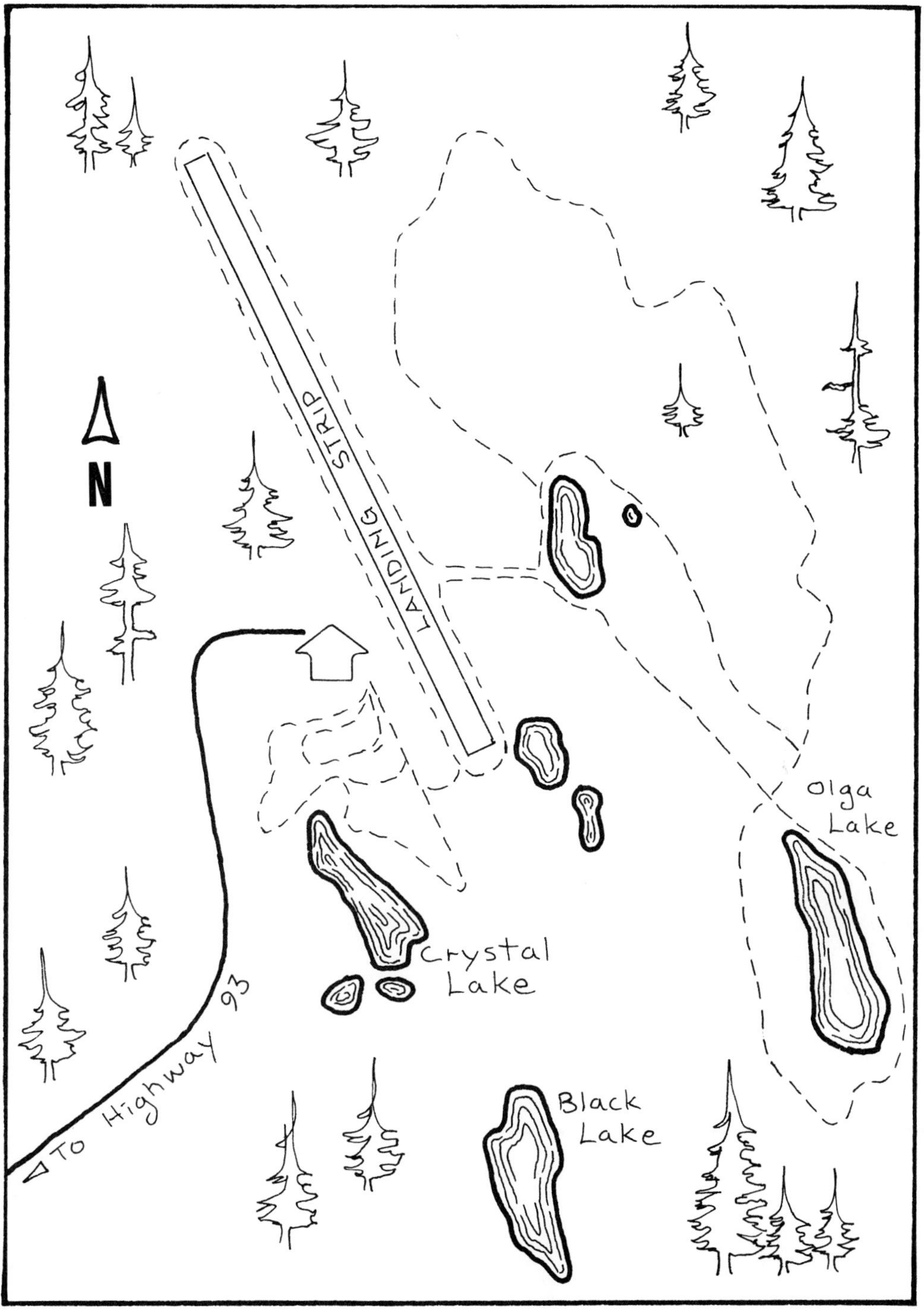
N
LANDING STRIP
Olga Lake
Crystal Lake
Black Lake
To Highway 93

Montana Sports Ranch

Location

1 mile west of Montana 83 on Guest Ranch Road; 80 miles south of Kalispell, 80 miles north of Missoula.

Accommodations

12 roomy units house 3 people each — total guest capacity 36. Each room has a double bed, day couch, private bath and gas heat. No kitchens. $35 per day includes all meals.

Services

Meals provided. Bar with hot-to-go pizza and sandwiches on premises. Gas and groceries on highway near ranch.

Trails and Snow Conditions

Ski on nearby roads or break your own trail through the woods and across open fields on the ranch property or in adjacent national forest. Temperatures typically in the teens and 20's; 150-200 inches of snow; elevation 3,800 feet.

Ski Rentals and Lessons

Ski rentals on premises. Lessons may be offered — inquire on current status.

Reservations

A few days notice needed for lodging. No credit cards. No pets.
Montana Sports Ranch
Condon, MT 59826
(406) 754-2351

Between the Bob Marshall Wilderness to the east and the Mission Mountains on the west, you'll find Montana Sports Ranch nestled in the valley.

When Ron and Candy Hummel bought the 240-acre guest ranch in the early 70's, they were faced with the task of weed-pulling and needed repairs brought on by three years of disuse. They pitched in, cleaned up and brought the ranch back to life. All the existing structures were there at the time they took over, but through the years, the Hummels have made their contributions. For example, the rustic furnishings — pine beds and chairs, cedar-topped tables — were handcrafted by Ron and Candy.

Though somewhat sparsely furnished, guest quarters are spacious and clean. The three separate buildings which house guest rooms are within immediate

Above: A young ski fan tests the powder near Montana Sports Ranch. Below: The on-premise "Ranch House Bar" is the original 1916 homestead cabin, now updated for use by guests and locals alike.

proximity of one another and of the "ranch kitchen", where you'll sit down at long tables with other tourers to partake of hearty and wholesome meals. Guests might include anyone from your next door neighbor to visitors from across the sea. You all will be able to don your skis at the door and glide around the ranch or practice telemarking on a little hill behind your breakfast stop.

The "Ranch House Bar", the on-premise drinking establishment, is what a Montana bar should look like. The separate structure is constructed of symmetrical 12-inch logs and was the original house on the 1916 homestead. Logs are chinked with mud on the exterior, and inside with pine wedges. Built as a two-story cabin, half the upstairs floor has been cut away to provide a loft and high ceiling. Donated mementos cover the wood walls: a "Montana mousetrap" (bear trap), "Montana fish hook" (logging chain), a 6-foot rattlesnake skin and various ranch implements.

A well-burnished horseshoe-shaped bar, complete with wooden "nails" in a bar-top groove, is the focal point of the room. Recreational pursuits are rounded out with pool table and juke box.

In addition to the virtually unlimited skiing possibilities at the ranch area, the forest service has identified several trails nearby. Red Butte, Cold Lake, Cold

Above: Indoor recreation awaits after a day of skiing. Proprietor Ron Hummel holds forth behind the horseshoe bar. Below: Touring on ranch pastureland requires the sharing of turf with four-legged residents.

Creek Drainage and Smith Creek trail information is available at the forest service office on Highway 83 just north of Guest Ranch Road.

For those who wish to venture farther, forest service trails are maintained at Jewell Basin, off Echo Lake Road, south of Bigfork.

Sports Ranch management offers pick-up service at no extra charge for guests arriving by air at Missoula or Kalispell, or by train at Whitefish.

Above: Montana Sports Ranch lies just beyond the turn-around for the county snow plow. Below: The whole neighborhood gang gets together for a good time on little-used roadways near the guest ranch.

Holland Lake Lodge

Location

4½ miles off Montana 83. 20 miles north of Seeley Lake, Montana; 45 miles north of Missoula.

Accommodations

Lodge rooms, with bath down hall, have either double or single beds. Lodge will house 22 overnight guests at $27.50 for 2. 3 cabins (each sleeps 4) will be winterized for '82-83 ski season. Rates are $40 per cabin with cooking facilities; $35 without.

Services

Restaurant and bar on premises; gas and groceries on highway nearby.

Trails and Snow Conditions

Marked trails, some packed, provide skiing for all ability levels. Choose from level terrain, woods, logging roads, a ridge route or an 8-mile around the lake summer horse trail. Elevation is 3,500 feet.

Ski Rentals and Lessons

No rentals. Lessons, including some snow survival instruction, may be provided by advance request.

Reservations

4 weeks ahead for groups; a few days smaller parties. Pick-up at Missoula airport or Whitefish rail stop, with extra charge, upon request. MC, Visa. Pets limited to cabins.

Holland Lake Lodge
Swan Valley Star Route
Condon, MT 59826
(406) 754-2282

Cozied against the eastern edge of the Swan River Valley is a "fantasy" inn on the shore of Holland Lake. At Holland Lake Lodge you can ski in an enchanted fairyland of a mid-winter's night dream. Your only distraction may be dodging the delicate white-tail deer which heavily populate the valley.

The tucked-away valley, still virtually undiscovered by ski tourers, lies between the Mission Mountains and the Swan Range just east of Flathead, the largest lake west of the Mississippi River. The valley is just 12 miles wide and it runs south for 50 miles from Bigfork, Montana.

The two-story lodge was built in 1947 to replace an original structure which burned. The resort had been operated traditionally for summer recreation — boating, horseback riding, packing, hiking — and opened in winter for the first time in 1980. Carole and Dick Schaeffer — with their two children — and Loris and Howard Uhl, all from Portland, Oregon, had heard about the availability of Holland Lake Lodge. After one look, they packed up and moved to Montana in May 1980.

The resort, located on national forest land, had fallen into disrepair. But the two families poured on the "409" and skillfully executed steel wool pads to transform the *truly* rustic log building into a shining jewel of burnished natural wood. Floors, railings and furniture are immaculate and virtually sparkle with the restoration cure.

There is something to view at every turn — from the split log stairway to the horseshoe coat rack.

Beautifully crafted furniture was hand honed by John Stark, a resident of

The narrow Swan River Valley east of Montana's Flathead Lake is the site of little-discovered ski touring country. Shoreline Holland Lake Lodge, recently opened for winter guests, offers wooded trails and deer sightings.

nearby Lindbergh Lake, who made almost all valley resort furniture from the 30's through the 50's.

The lake and nearby 9,350-foot Holland Peak were named for Ben Holland, first person to settle between Swan and Seeley Lakes — which he did in the mid-1880's. The local area has a rich history of legend and lore — ask Loris to tell you how Dr. Gordon acquired the ranch and what the Holland Lake massacre was all about.

Meals at Holland Lake Lodge are fast food breakfasts and lunches (*do* try the Gut Bomb, a 7-inch hamburger) and family-style dinners. Dinner is by reservation only — let Howard or someone know by 2 p.m. Every Friday is burger night from 5-9. Sack lunches are available to take along on the trail.

This is one *special* place. Once it's discovered, get in line!

The main lodge at Holland Lake has been polished to a knat's eye by new owners. Guest rooms are inviting and several cabins have been winterized. Meals are available in the light and airy log main lodge.

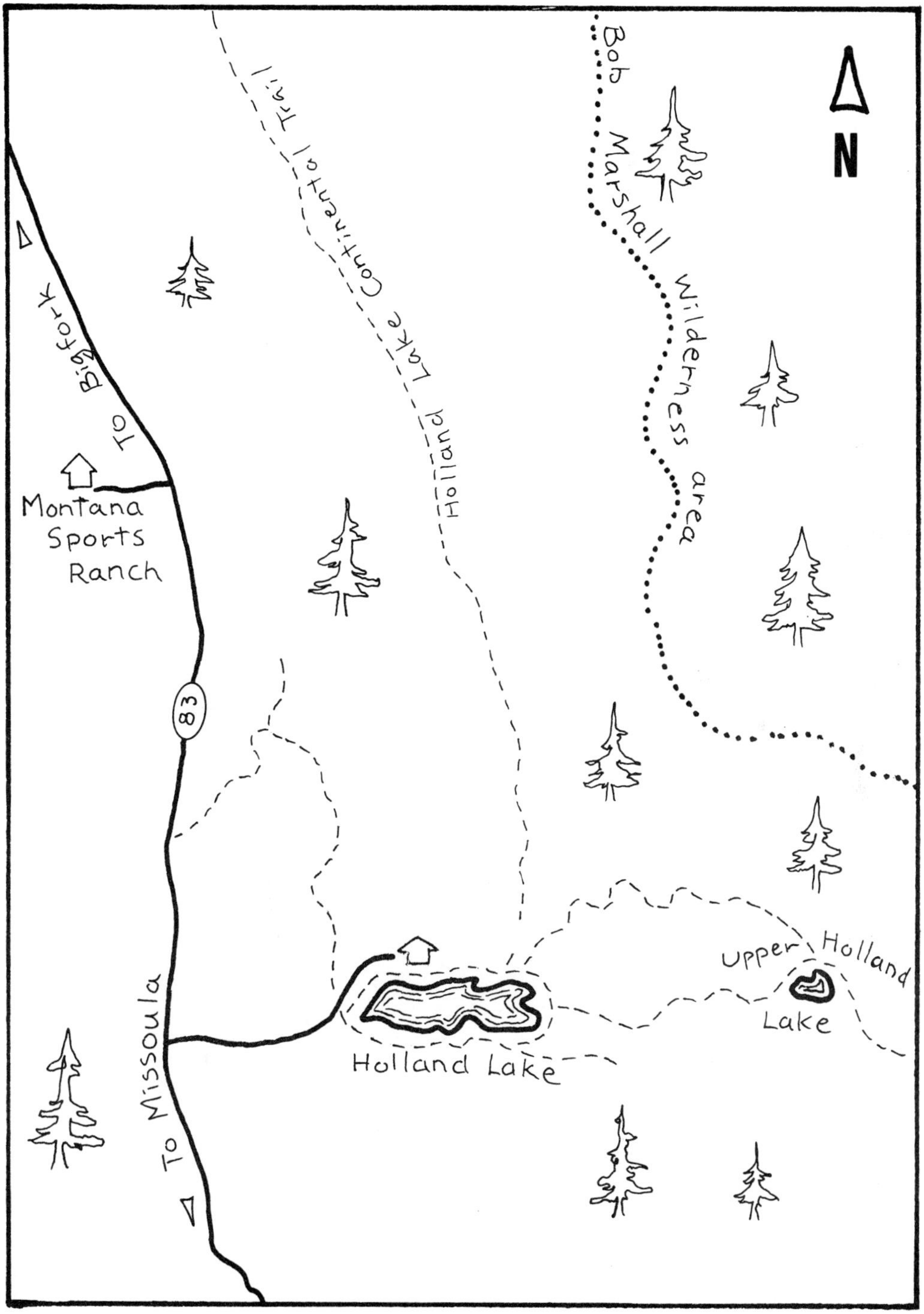
N
Bob Marshall Wilderness area
Holland Lake Continental Trail
To Bigfork
Montana
Sports
Ranch
83
To Missoula
Holland Lake
Upper Holland
Lake

Lolo Hot Springs Resort

Location
On U.S. 12, 7 miles east of Lolo Pass/Idaho border. 36 miles west of Missoula, Montana.

Accommodations
Accommodations for 35 people at the resort's old Mineral Springs Hotel. 1 cabin with kitchen, double and single bed arrangements; share bath. Sleeping bags on floor okay. $19 up per unit. 4 motel units at main resort have private baths, no kitchens. 7 primitive cabins (no water, no indoor facilities, no dishes, no bedding). Main resort rates start at $18. Group discounts available.

Services
Restaurant, bar, gas, groceries, indoor and outdoor pools at main resort; indoor hot plunge at old hotel.

Trails and Snow Conditions
Miles of marked trails on forest service land immediately adjacent to resort. One trail follows an old bob sled run. Maps and information at resort or at visitors' center at the pass.

Ski Rentals and Lessons
No rentals or lessons.

Reservations
For hotel lodging, book at least one month in advance for weekends and holidays.
Lolo Hot Springs Resort
Lolo, MT 59847
Phone Missoula operator, ask for Lolo #1

Just down the highway from Lolo Hot Springs main resort is an old hotel nestled in a glen, with a hot spring of its own. The Mineral Springs Hotel has been doing business for a long time, but relatively few people know about it.

Of the winter guests staying in the area, about 75% are xc skiers, 25% are snowmobilers. The skiers usually choose to stay at the hotel.

Guests visiting either location in winter may use any of the area's three hot pools at no extra charge. At the hotel, the clean indoor plunge has a water temperature of 104°. The hotel and concrete dressing room floors are geothermally heated.

The quaint old structure, with unpeeled cedars in the lobby supporting the second story, was built in the mid 20's. Waters at the spa often are sought for therapeutic purposes. There is a faint odor of sulphur upon the air.

Resort operators encourage use of the facilities by church groups. Plans are now underway for expansion of overnight accommodations and for development of additional traveler services.

Ski touring conditions in this Bitterroot Range location are excellent with magnificent snow, generally crisp sunny days, and a variety of trails from which to choose. Loop trails of varying distances,

Old Mineral Springs Hotel, part of Lolo Hot Springs Resort, is a popular overnight stop for ski tourers seeking to take the waters. Both the indoor plunge at the hotel and the hot pools at the main resort are free to guests.

one-way car shuttles, and wooded trails near the resort offer something for everyone.

At the top of Lolo Pass, on the Idaho/Montana border, stop at the visitor's center to pick up forest service maps and current trail information. Recreational Opportunity Guides (ROG's) for cross country skiing, thoroughly detailed tour maps, are available locally. The printed one or two-page information sheets gradually are being standardized and put into use by U.S. national forests. They include specifics on highway access, marking systems, and terrain and elevation data, complete with cross-section line charts.

Though not yet in widespread use, the trail guides are available in many Montana forest service offices.

Above, top: Lolo guests are sometimes welcomed by inquisitive locals. Above: Accommodations range from primitive cabin to motel unit to hotel room. Below: The resort complex near Lolo Pass includes restaurant and bar room.

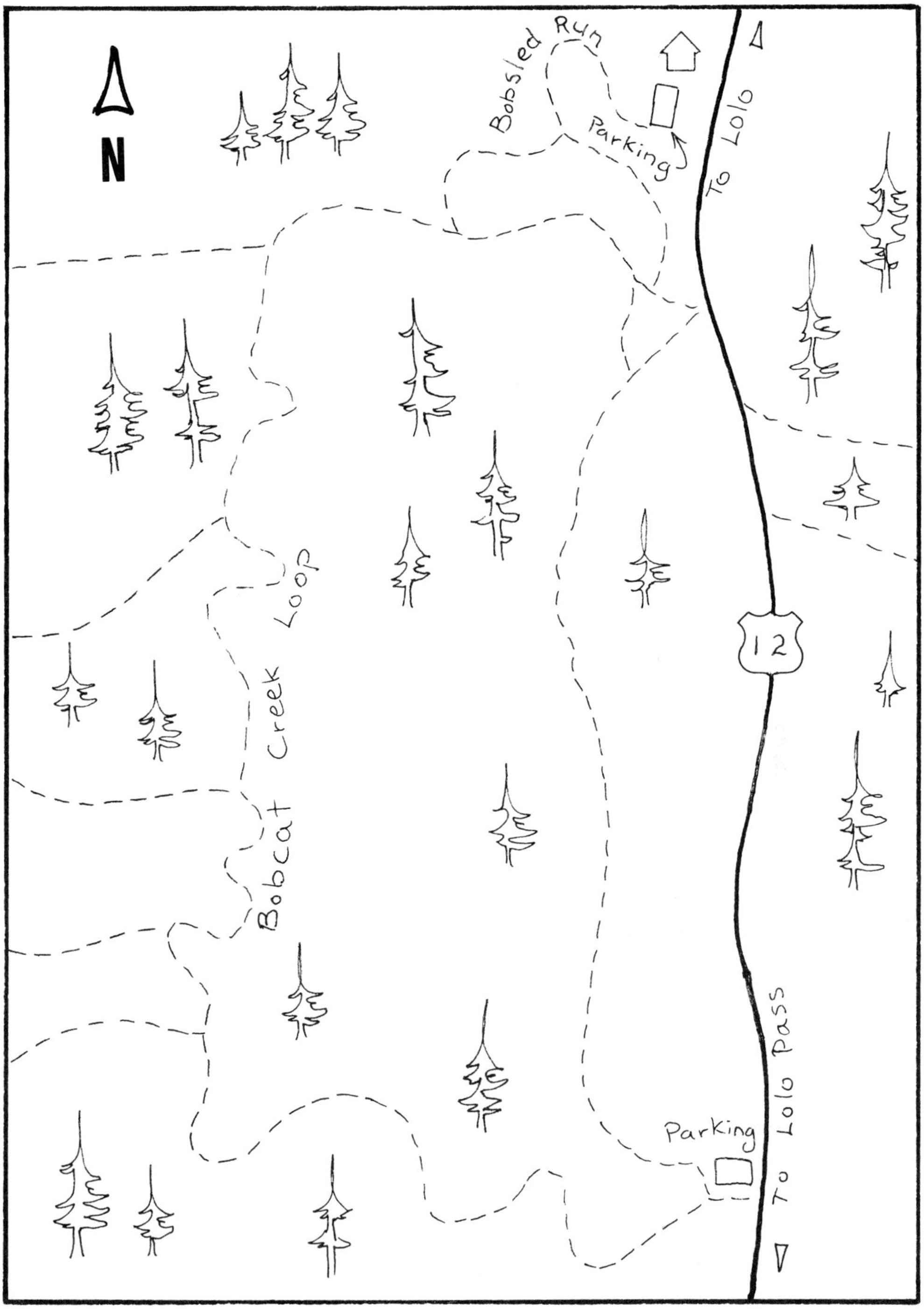

N
Bobsled Run
Parking
To Lolo
Bobcat Creek Loop
12
Parking
To Lolo Pass

Sleeping Child Hot Springs Resort

Location
At the end of county road 501, 10½ miles off U.S. 93; 13 miles southeast of Hamilton, Montana; 57 miles south of Missoula.

Accommodations
5 units in A-frame lodge accommodate a total of 18 in beds. Maximum 6 people per room. All units have private baths. The suite has kitchenette, Jacuzzi, color TV. Rates $36-49 double occupancy; $6 per extra person in room. 24-hour pool privileges included in room rate.

Services
Restaurant, bar, sauna, two 24-hour outdoor hot pools. Groceries and gas at Hamilton.

Trails and Snow Conditions
Skiing on trails and unplowed roads on forest service land near resort. Skiing ability level — advanced. Skiers are cautioned to stay on trails and check with the forest service at Darby for information on conditions. Elevation 5,000 feet.

Ski Rentals and Lessons
Rentals available at Hamilton ski shops.

Reservations
MC, Visa. No pets.
Sleeping Child Hot Springs Resort
Box 768
Hamilton, MT 59840
(406) 363-9910

When Chief Joseph led his Nez Perce followers northeasterly, fleeing toward Canada with the U.S. Army hot in pursuit, he found it necessary to stop periodically for battle. When they reached these hot springs, the Indians were obliged to leave their tired children to rest by the warm waters while they went off to skirmish with the cavalry. When the adults returned, the children were still nodding off, secure as when the parents left them. Hence the name Sleeping Child Hot Springs.

Joel Chopot, manager of the Bitterroot Valley resort, points out a rock formation in front of the modern lodge which, when viewed without its snow cover, resembles the resort's sleeping child logo. Joel prefers the rock-picture theory as to the origin of the christening.

The sleeping child theme is carried out even to a stone outline of the logo on the tile floor in front of the lodge fireplace.

An early owner of the spa renamed it "Eureka." But the title didn't stick and was quickly reverted to Sleeping Child.

For awhile, the hot springs had a ghost wandering about. Former owner George Loftus went off on a hunting trip in the late 50's and never returned. Seven years later, his skeleton was found, but the cause of his death never determined.

End of the road retreat, Sleeping Child Hot Springs Resort, lies in a snug pocket in Montana's Sapphire Mountains, east of the Bitterroot Valley. The lodge provides immediate access to mountainous trails.

It has been reported that George's spirit used to visit the lodge, and even now, on a moonlit night, when the mists rise from the hot pools. . . .

Skiing in the rocky steep-sided canyon areas near the resort is difficult, and recommended only for experienced skiers. Be sure you know where you are going (tell someone) and consult with the forest service for information on such areas as Two Bear and White Stallion trails.

Groomed trails are available at Lost Horse Nordic Village (see separate listing).

Above: Lodge "pent house", the Raven's Nest, offers spiffy accommodations and a balcony overlooking the hot pools. Below: Indoor diversions at Sleeping Child include wide-screen TV, Pac Man and pool.

If it turns out that the snow is too deep and the trail too steep, come on back to the lodge. There are such recreational pursuits as pool, videogames and wide-screen TV. Take your beverage out by the hot water pools for some mighty good therapy.

This is a beautiful, special place. Reserve the "Raven's Nest" at the top of the lodge for a snug retreat. This hide-away rests at the very apex of the three-story A-frame lodge, has an out-side balcony overlooking the hot pools, and like other lodge units, is comfortably furnished and immaculate.

A sauna and 24-hour hot pools guarantee immediate warmth after a ski outing — even on the coldest of winter days. The completely enclosed pool area adjacent to the lodge building is fed by natural hot springs.

Lost Horse Nordic Village

Location

4 miles west of U.S. 93 at the end of Lost Horse Road, 12½ miles southwest of Hamilton, Montana.

Accommodations

2 cabins sleep 2 and 4 persons each. Smaller cabin has a hot tub. No water or toilets in cabins. Rest room and shower facilities in main lodge building. Sleeping bags suggested for cold nights. Cabin rates $25 and $40, double occupancy.

Services

Fast food service available after 2 p.m. Lighted tubing hill, sauna, bar on premises. Gas and groceries at Darby or Hamilton.

Trails and Snow Conditions

10-15 kilometers machine-set tracts on loop trails through woods and open areas and along creek beds. 60 miles additional trails, sometimes machine packed, on premises and bordering national forest land. Snow coach trips may be arranged to transport you 8 or 13 miles from lodge for an all-downhill return. Fee dependent upon distance.

Ski Rentals and Lessons

Complete rental service, ski accessories and lessons, wax room at Snow Goose Nordic shop on premises. All ability levels taught — both private and group (limited to 10) lessons available by advance arrangement.

Reservations

Book several months ahead for weekends and holidays; no problem on weekdays. No credit cards. Dogs restricted to roadways.

Lost Horse Nordic Village
Attn: Randy
P.O. Box 1116
Hamilton, MT 59840
(406) 363-1516 or 777-5770

Something exciting happens every weekend at Lost Horse Nordic Village.

Owners Randy Hodgson and Bob and Judy Cameron schedule a list of winter events at Lost Horse Nordic that would mind-boggle the most compulsive of list-makers. They include a variety of xc races, fun days, skijoring (dog tow), special Olympics, and a number of sled dog competitions including the start and finish ceremonies for the 520-mile, nine-day Montana State Sled Dog Championships.

The "village" is a privately-owned complex of xc trails and historic buildings, one of which houses what has been described as "the most unique saloon in Montana." Be prepared for a *most unique* sight before you enter. The chinked logs of the 1865 house provide a backdrop for the wildest array of decor items and mementos you've ever seen. Over the bar hangs a well-antlered, snarling deer head with special dentures — the fangs of a large carnivore. There are traps, rattlesnake skins, license plates, a horse hoof complete with iron shoe, harness parts — and squeezed in between everything else are more than 900 dollar bills (and some foreign currency) signed and left by customers.

Bob, original proprietor of all this craziness and wonderment, invested in the property as a base for mountain photography and pack trips. He moved the saloon building down from Townsend to serve as his headquarters.

Nebraska transplant Randy, who had become temporarily sidetracked in Missoula on a post-grad trip through the

Guest cabins at Lost Horse Nordic Village have seen many a cold Montana winter. The 19th century buildings were moved to the touring center a few years ago. The older of the two was constructed of square logs in 1830.

West, came out to ski at Bob's place in November 1978. The rest is history. With Randy's Nordic interest and expertise, the two developed trails, set up a ski shop and brought two more log structures to the area for guest use.

Randy is extremely active with local ski activities. Not only does he donate one day each per week to the Bill Koch Youth Ski League and a group of mentally handicapped skiers, but he also teaches at local xc ski clinics and is an active member of the Nordic Ski Patrol.

This area is rich in the history of the Lewis and Clark expedition. The Nordic Village takes its name from the fact that the explorers lost a horse near here.

You will have marvelous snow and ski conditions at this 4,100-foot location, as well as the unbeatable scenery of Montana's Bitterroot country. An extensive and varied trail system provides something for every Nordic skier. Use of all trails is free to lodge guests. Several miles of machine-set tracks loop through the woods around the Village, and a variety of touring choices lead up creek bed trails and summer ridge roads for spectacular views of the Bitterroot Range.

The accommodations are not luxurious, to be sure. But if you like authenticity in your log housing and don't mind roughing it a bit, you'll love Lost Horse. The older of the two cabins, built in 1830, is constructed of square logs and now has a sleeping loft and a modern hot tub which helps make up for any cold-night discomfort. The two cabins are adequately furnished, very quaint, and the smaller one is a cozy hideaway for a couple. And they do provide you with immediate access to all that glorious ski terrain.

Newcomers to the Lost Horse saloon may be momentarily startled by the vicious-looking deer head behind the bar. Once recovered, they will find hours of study material upon the walls and ceilings of the old log house.

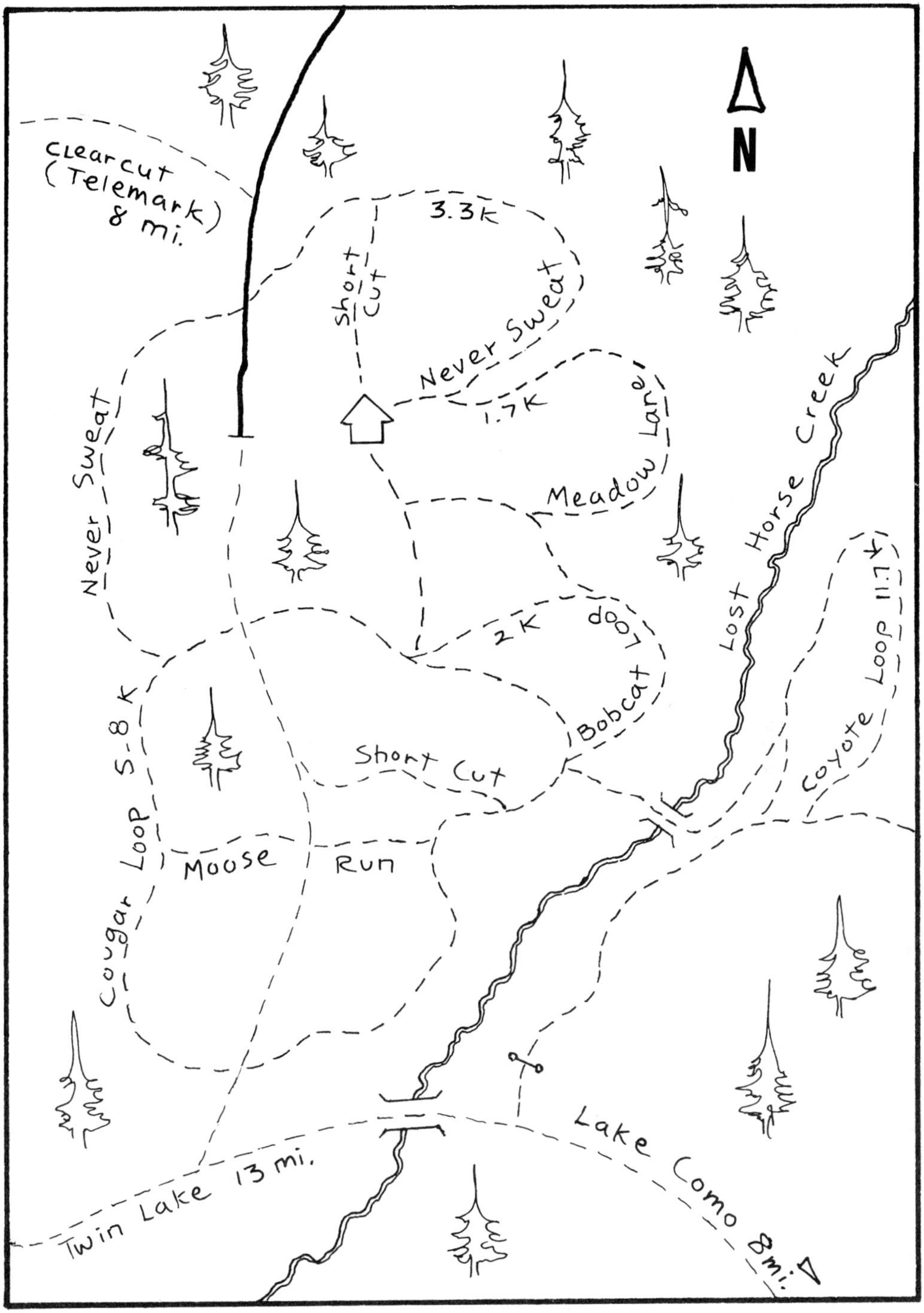
N
Clearcut (Telemark) 8 mi.
3.3K
Short Cut
Never Sweat
1.7K
Meadow Lane
Never Sweat
Lost Horse Creek
2K
Bobcat Loop
Coyote Loop 11.1K
Cougar Loop 5.8K
Short Cut
Moose Run
Lake Como 8 mi.
Twin Lake 13 mi.

Lost Trail Hot Springs Resort

Location
On U.S. 93, 88 miles south of Missoula, Montana; 44 miles south of Hamilton; 56 miles north of Salmon, Idaho.

Accommodations
Cabins and rooms in 3 lodges accommodate 135 people. Lodge facilities range from dorm-style bunk beds to modern units with lofts and cooking facilities; private or shared baths. Most bath facilities are toilet and sink only — showers at hot pools. Cabins are available in various sizes and some have fully-equipped kitchens. Bedding and towels are included with lodging except bring sleeping bags for bunks. Rates start at $8 per night on a 4-night basis in a bunk, to $45/night for a cabin. Meals can be included on weekends for an additional $10 per day.

Services
Restaurant, bar, outdoor pool, indoor sauna and whirlpool — open Friday-Sunday. Suit rentals 50¢. Gas and grocieries 6 miles north at Sula.

Trails and Snow Conditions
17½ kilometers machine-set tracks on national forest land. Additional xc skiing 6 miles south at Lost Trail Downhill Ski Area. One-ride lift ticket, $1.50. Typical winter temperature, 15-20 degrees.

Ski Rentals and Lessons
Rentals, lessons, guided tours by advance reservation on weekends.

Reservations
MC, Visa. Pets allowed in cabins or on leash on grounds. Reserve weekends 2 weeks ahead, longer for holidays.
Lost Trail Hot Springs Resort
Box 37
Sula, MT 59871
(406) 821-3574

In September 1805, the Lewis and Clark expedition left the Salmon, Idaho, area and headed north for the Bitterroot Valley. Near the Divide, their Indian guide missed Moose Creek Trail, the planned route, and led the party up Fish Creek, adding another arduous day to the climb.

The altered journey brought them down Camp Creek. Then, tuckered out, the group rested for two days at Ross' Hole. The way became known, appropriately enough, as "Lost Trail."

Today the route is well marked, and you can travel along Camp Creek on your skis. But forget Ross' Hole — stay at the hot springs resort.

Tucked away in the trees alongside Camp Creek, close to the Montana/Idaho border, is Lost Trail Hot Springs Resort. For 20 years prior to 1977 it was operated as a private kids' camp.

Then Alaskans Dick and Stella Powers bought the complex. The couple owns a general store at Angoon, on Admiralty Island, and learned it was most difficult to run a resort in Montana while residing out of state.

In Yakatat, they met Tom and Kathy Nichols. At that time, Tom was an Alaska state game warden — a transplanted forest ranger from Salmon, Idaho — and he was ready not only to leave government service, but to return to the lower 48 as well. In April 1979, the foursome formed a partnership and the Nichols family moved to Lost Trail to assume management of the resort.

One of several lodges at Lost Trail Resort provides guests with a choice of double-bed room or bunks. Other overnight housing includes loft-style lodge rooms, with or without cooking facilities, and complete cabins.

Then another symbiosis took place. In 1981, Don Garramone, a Missoula carpenter, was doing some work at the resort. One fall afternoon after work, as he basked in the hot pool, he mentioned to Tom, "You ought to have cross country skiing here."

Tom replied, "Why don't you do it?"

That summit meeting formed what is becoming an extensive and well-run xc program at Lost Trail.

The Nordic effort got underway at Thanksgiving time that year, and now Don and Carol Majeske trek down from Missoula every Saturday morning to set fresh tracks and serve as on-site xc hosts and instructors.

Part of the program includes a winter carnival. In February, the resort is the scene of snow sculpture, tubing, crazy-ski relays and hot pool volleyball.

Skiing in the vicinity is excellent. The powder is so fine it will break your little skier's heart. Currently 17½ kilometers of trails are marked and set with more to come.

On the resort trails, a lovely choice for a ski picnic is the West Camp Creek Campground area. It's a short tour and you can relax for lunch in full sun. If you're waxing, and you ski the 4-kilometer route at Waugh Gulch, go to the left instead of right at the cattle guard. The first uphill is in the shade, and then a gradual downhill glide is sunny.

An all-day option with car shuttle is to drive to the Lost Trail Ski Area, hop on the boards and ski for five hours back to the resort — downhill all the way. Let

What more luxurious way to end a day of rigorous ski touring than with a fresh-air swim or soak in a natural hot springs pool? Adjacent to the restaurant/lounge, the pool complex also offers an indoor Jacuzzi.

someone know where you are going. If you're not familiar with the area, getting lost is a distinct possibility.

Elevation at the base of the lifts is 7,200 feet; at the resort, 5,600.

Lodging choices run from bunks to fully-furnished housekeeping cabins; from rustic to contemporary. Facilities are winterized and carefully maintained.

For evening entertainment, there is usually live music in the homey restaurant lounge. Or perhaps you'd prefer a moonlight tour. Better yet, grab a friend and head for a hot water soak.

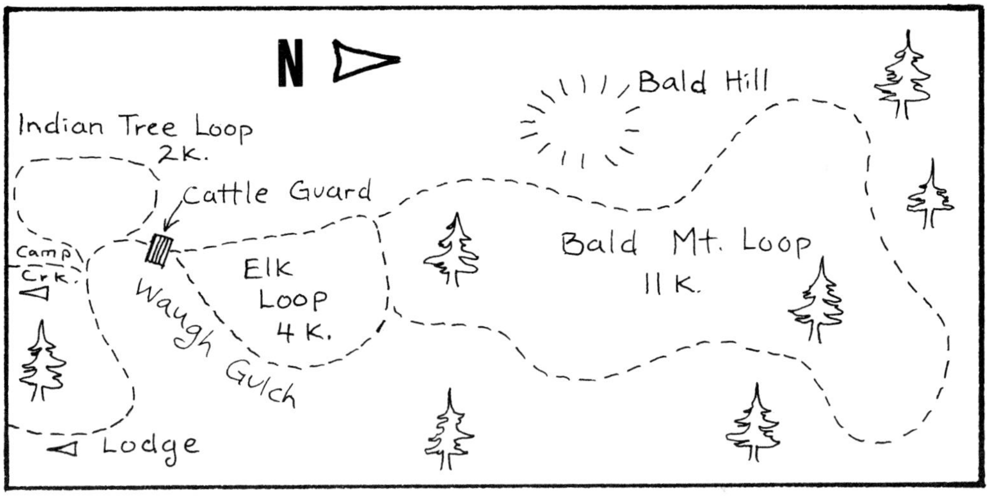

An easy tour through West Camp Creek Campground leads the Bitterroot Mountains tourer into Lewis and Clark expedition country. Fine snow conditions may be found on marked trails adjacent to Lost Trail Resort and in nearby areas.

Jackson Hot Springs

Location
At Jackson, on Montana 278. 48 miles west of Dillon.

Accommodations
18 cabins with fireplaces and full baths, plus 4 "apartments" with ½ bath and central shower can accommodate 2 to 4 people each — total capacity, 62. No kitchens. Rates start at $24.

Services
Bar, hot pool with $1 swimsuit rentals at lodge; gas, groceries, restaurant in immediate vicinity.

Trails and Snow Conditions
6,400 foot elevation provides snow at the door. Forest service trails are within easy driving access. Lodge proprietors will transport skiers by snow machine to any of several destinations for a one-way downhill tour back to the lodge. Fee corresponds to distance of ride. Get maps from forest service office at Wisdom, 18 miles northwest.

Ski Rentals and Lessons
No ski instruction or rentals are available locally.

Reservations
Jackson Hot Springs Lodge
P.O. Box 808
Jackson, MT 59736
(406) 834-2141

Jackson Montana, is a town where you don't have to look before crossing the road. Virtually one street wide, the community sprawls for about two blocks down Highway 278.

The log lodge, with its monster icicles hanging down from steam pouring out of the hot pool building, rests in the heart of town. Just across the street are the U.S. post office, the gas pump, and Rose's Cantina. When asked the population of Jackson, spa co-owner Jenny Humphrey responds, "50, counting the cats and dogs people leave when they move out."

Jenny and her husband Glenn bought the hot springs lodge in 1977 and made extensive repairs to the 1950 vintage structures. In February 1982 they leased the operation to Minnesota transplants, Ben and Jenny Pauley. The Pauleys' youngest son, Joe, increased the local two-room elementary school population from 10 to 11 when he enrolled in Jackson's seventh grade.

There are no guest rooms in the lodge — the warm wood building is dominated by a huge dance floor, 28′ x 46′, which serves as the main entry to the structure. The "Diamond Bar" at one end of the

The big log lodge at Jackson, Montana, features an enormous ballroom and indoor hot springs pool. The lodge faces tiny Jackson's one main street and is adjacent to town services. Overnight housing is in roomy cabins.

enormous room provides friendly atmosphere, $1 drinks and such posted admonitions as, "In case of air raid, hide under the men's urinal — it never gets hit."

Adjacent to the lodge is a 30′ x 75′ "swimming pool" with water temperature cooled to about 95 degrees. Use of the pool is free to lodge guests.

The hot mineral water comes out of the ground at 137 degrees, 1,300 feet above the lodge, and has enough gravity flow pressure to supply the hot springs complex without use of a pump. Glenn installed natural hot water heat into the main lodge building after taking over operation of the facilities.

Water is so hot in the cabins that ice is provided free to guests to cool down their drinking water. There may be no cold tap water, so showering can be a blistering experience. Hint: poke holes in the bottom of your ice bag, hang bag on shower head and let hot water melt ice onto you as you shower. No guarantees.

Knotty pine cabins are roomy, beds are comfortable and such built-ins as tiny

Above: Cowboying, Big Hole style, is accomplished with a herd dog and snow machines. Below: The immense two-story ballroom in Jackson Hot Springs Lodge serves as entry to bar, registration desk and swimming pool.

benches in fireplace alcoves make staying here a bit more cozy and inviting than your basic Holiday Inn.

Although you can ski virtually anywhere in the Big Hole Basin, where Jackson nestles, a run up Warm Springs Creek drainage will bring you to such trail areas as Woody, Jackson and Little Milk Creeks.

This country is known as "The Land of 10,000 Haystacks" and you'll see lots of cattle and snow-covered hay fields hereabouts. If you drive down Highway 43 west from Wisdom, you'll come to the Big Hole Battlefield, a monument operated by the National Park Service. The facilities are located on the site of an 1877 Nez Perce encampment, and scene of one of the battles along Chief Joseph's flight route.

At Wisdom, *the* place to eat is Fetty's and across the street at the Antlers Bar (every Montana town west of the Divide has an Antlers Bar) a window sign proclaims "Liquor in front, poker in reer."

Should you require additional entertainment on your visit to Jackson, ask "town mayor" Whiskey Bill about the night the sled dog teams stayed in town. You may find him at Rose's Cantina.

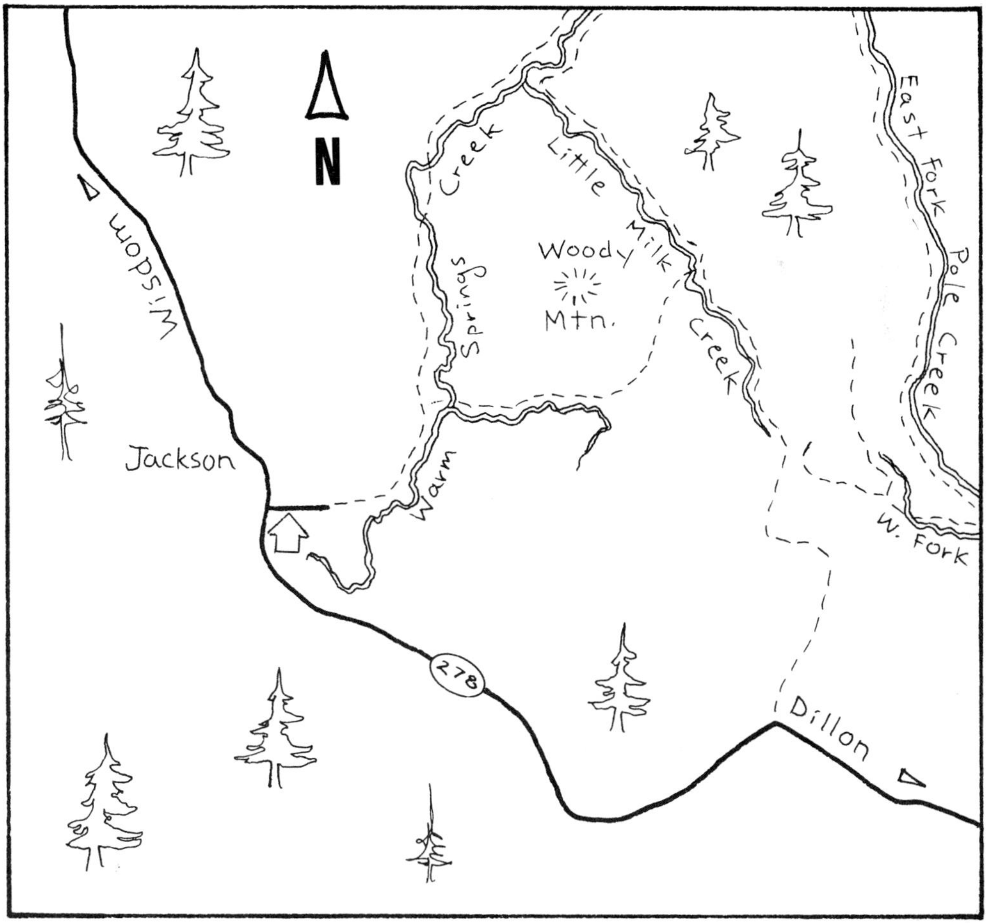

Elkhorn Hot Springs Resort

Location

On Elkhorn/Polaris Road, 13 miles north of Montana 278; 43 miles west of Dillon; 100 miles south of Butte.

Accommodations

Resort can accommodate approximately 60 people in primitive cabins with kitchens, wood heat; some with fireplaces. In winter there is no water in the cabins, and toilet facilities are outdoors. Although bedding, towels and wood are provided, guests are advised to bring sleeping bags in below zero weather. A few rooms in the lodge (bath down the hall) may be ready for winter 1982-83. Rates start at $16 for 2.

Services

Restaurant, beer, wine, gas, limited groceries, 2 outdoor hot pools, 2 indoor Grecian saunas on the premises.

Trails and Snow Conditions

30 kilometers of machine-set tracks, cooperatively maintained by resort, forest service and the Beaverhead XC Ski Club. All trails are well-marked and provide a loop access system on virtually all terrain options for every ability level, from 7,400 to 8,300 feet. Non-maintained trails access additional mountain areas.
Snow depth, 4 to 8 feet.

Ski Rentals and Lessons

No lessons available locally. The resort may stock rentals next year.

Reservations

Allow 3 weeks lead time for weekend reservations, 3 months for holidays. Weekdays and the month of April, no problem.
Elkhorn Hot Springs
P.O. Box 514
Polaris, MT 59746
(406) 834-2416

The Compleat Touring Experience. That's what you'll get at Elkhorn Hot Springs Resort in Montana's Beaverhead Range. Set tracks, hot pools, quaint cabins, rustic lodge, mountain scenery — they have it all.

On groomed trails, ski to Solarium Point for an overlook of the Grasshopper Valley or tour to 8,300 feet and view the Gallatin Range. Be prepared for a view of moose *anywhere* on the trails.

Off the marked routes, the more experienced skier may want to break trail to the top of 10,212-foot Comet Mountain, a 13-mile round trip.

Adventurous tourers, here is your chance to ski to and spend the night in a ghost town. A hefty 22-mile round trip tour will take you to Coolidge City, where activity once bustled at the old Elkhorn Mine. Skiers may find shelter in abandoned town site buildings. Between 1914-1929, 21 families lived in Coolidge City where gold and silver were mined as well as processed before being shipped.

Additional ski variety may be found at nearby Maverick Mountain where $2 will get you a ride to the top for telemarking back down on Remley Run.

The main lodge, a large, beautiful rustic affair, was built in 1924. When Bernal and Jackie Kahrs bought it in 1980, the structure was condemned. In a short period of time, they have completely updated the facility and they are making great strides toward completion of their goals for the entire complex.

One of the amenities awaiting Elkhorn Hot Springs Resort guests is a selection of indoor and outdoor hot pools. Other delights are a charming old lodge and an excellent system of maintained loop trails.

"Would you believe I wore a three-piece business suit and carried a brief case?" asks former Archway Cookie Company general manager Kahrs. He was based in Seattle, he had overall responsibility for Archway's Northwest territory and decided he'd already made it to the top. When the Elkhorn opportunity surfaced, he and Jackie made their move.

One additional comment on the offerings — snowmobiles share the turf. The machines use the road past the lodge, the drivers stay in cabins and eat in the restaurant. But there the twain ends. Recreational trails are totally separated and problems are virtually non-existent.

On your way out from your stay at Elkhorn, *be sure* to allow enough time to stop at Polaris for a toddy at the Polar Bar. You can't miss it — it's the white frame building across the road from the ancient log post office, which once served as a boarding house at nearby Polaris Mine.

Polar John is your host at the informal one-room wayside, famous for the saga of John's johns and the May '81 600-person protest against government closure of John's establishment. It seems John has no running water in the bar and the restrooms are outdoors, both no-no's in the sanitarian's code book. Popular appeal and possibly a grandfather clause saved the day. John is doing business as usual, without the redundant trappings of big-city rules. As for sanitation, John's crone Walt, husband of Polaris' postmistress comments, "I've been coming in here for 35 years and I'm still alive." Six hundred people can't be wrong. And besides, The Polar Bar has got to be the last holdout of the 75¢ drink.

The Polar Bar at Polaris, Montana, is an unassuming structure, but definitely more modern than the town's other building, a 19th century log house which now serves as the post office. John's john is at left.

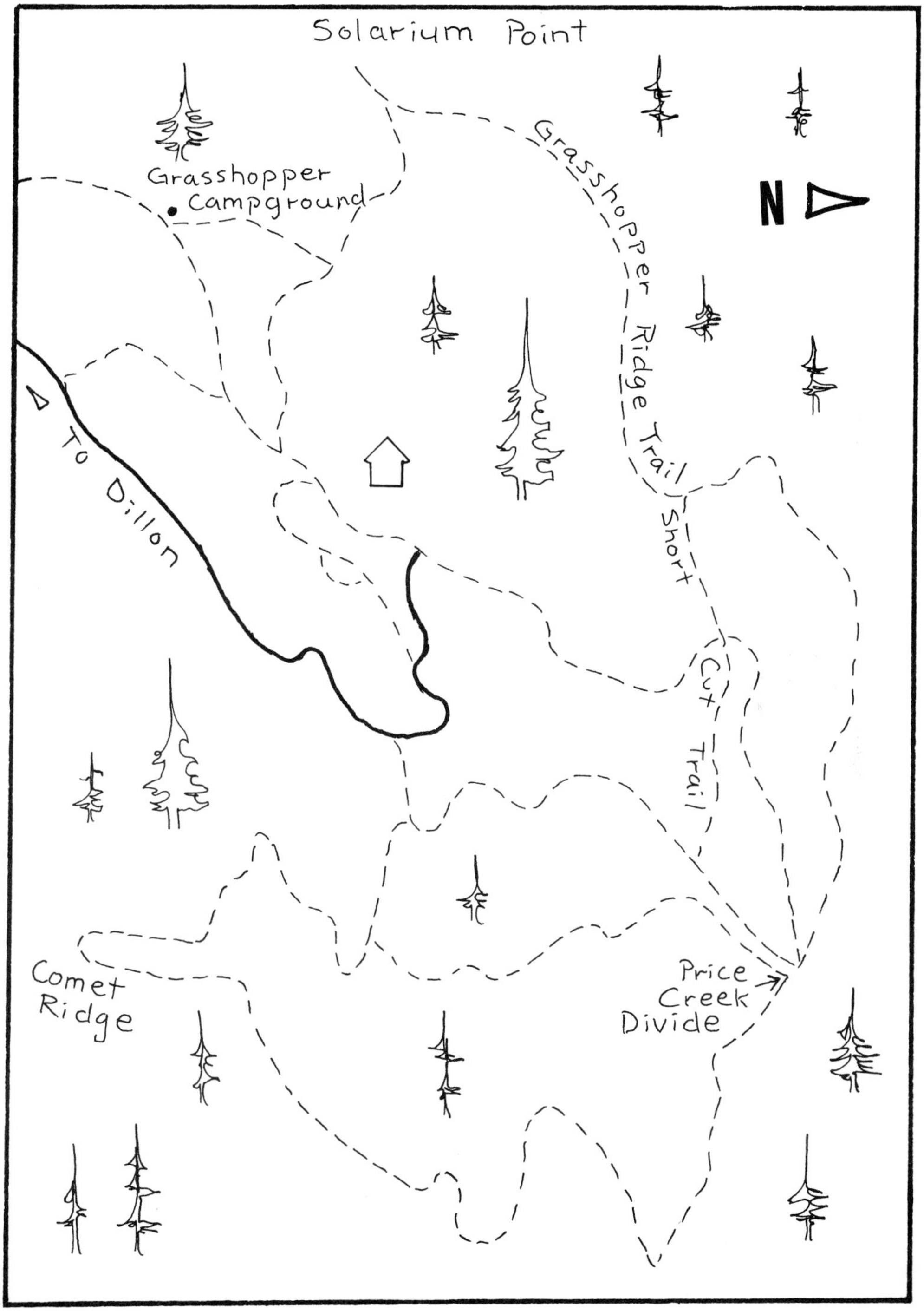
Solarium Point
Grasshopper Campground
Grasshopper Ridge Trail
N
To Dillon
Short Cut Trail
Comet Ridge
Price Creek Divide

Fairmont Hot Springs

Location
3 miles south of I-90; 15 miles west of Butte, Montana; 10 miles east of Anaconda.

Accommodations
170 hotel rooms, all with private baths, sleep 3 to 4 people each. No kitchens. Although summer rates start at $44 per room, inquire about varying winter specials.

Services
Dining room, coffee shop, lounge, 4 hot pools, gift shop on premises. Groceries and gas 3 miles west at Opportunity.

Trails and Snow Conditions
Several miles of trails on public land, some machine-packed, may be accessed 1 mile from resort. Some trails are shared with snowmobiles. The Anaconda, Georgetown Lake, Philipsburg areas offer an extensive variety of both marked and unmarked trails, all relatively unused.

Ski Rentals and Lessons
Ski rentals available at Peterson's Corral at main trail head 1 mile south of hot springs. Lessons and rentals at Discovery Basin, 28 miles west. Daily shuttle to Discovery Basin picks up passengers at hotel; $4 round trip.

Reservations
Book well in advance for weekends. Airport pickup at Butte available. Am Ex, MC Visa.
Fairmont Hot Springs
Anaconda, MT 59711
(406) 797-3241

The mile-high spa was once called Gregson Hot Springs. Local residents used it as a recreation area and they rode the train from nearby Butte and Anaconda to picnic on the grounds, dance in the ballroom and soak in hot mineral water.

As has happened with many old-time resort areas, Gregson fell into disuse and disrepair.

In 1974 it was replaced by all-new facilities and local developers called in the proprietor of British Columbia's Fairmont Hot Springs to do the job right. The seasoned resort operator came to the Montana spa on a 20-year lease basis, then purchased it within a few years.

Today's complex is a rambling, modern two-story hotel with the amenities of a big-city conference center. But few conference centers have a network of hot pools. Here you'll find two Olympic-size swimming pools, one outdoors, one in; and two 105-degree soaking pools.

The spring water surfaces at 160 degrees just outside the hotel and is capped for safety. The hotel is heated by hot water.

For the xc skier, one of the best facets of Fairmont is its access to beautiful and varied touring areas. In addition to a system at nearby Peterson's Corral, trails have been designated in Deerlodge National Forest, west of historic Anaconda.

At 6,300-foot Georgetown Lake in the Pintlar Mountains, a virtual ski paradise awaits discovery. During Anaconda's annual February snowfest, the lake area

Two glorious outdoor hot pools with a view of Montana's Continental Divide country are features of Fairmont. Another Olympic-size plunge and smaller soaking pool are indoors.

is the site of xc and downhill races, ice skating competition and horse-drawn cutter races. Georgetown Lake is also the scene of salmon and trout ice fishing.

Pintlar Mountains town Philipsburg also offers several marked trail systems. Information is available just south of town at the friendliest forest service office in three states. Philipsburg is a one-traffic-light town. Instructions for drivers: stop on red, wait on yellow, go on pink.

Anaconda is in a state of transition these days since the only show in town, the copper smelter, closed its doors in 1981. About 2,000 of the town's 10,000 residents had to move on, and the survivors are now in the business of developing tourism. A grant from the departing industry is helping to assure success of the effort, and the historic area offers much in the way of outdoor recreation and placid beauty.

Should you seek lodging a bit closer to the Deerlodge Forest trails, a small motel is open year around at 3,000-acre Georgetown Lake. The Brown Derby, on U.S. 10-A at the east end of the frozen lake, has seven units. The restaurant and its cozy log bar are open every day except Monday. Rates are $18 single, $20 double. All rooms have two double beds. Phone (406) 563-5072 or write Brown Derby, Georgetown Lake, Anaconda, MT 59711.

Meals are available daily at rustic Dentons Point on the south shore of the lake. Turn left at the first plowed road past the Brown Derby to reach Dentons.

Winter guests at Fairmont resort will find a number of diversions: dining room, lounge, natural hot springs, complete conference facilities, gift shop . . . and cross country skiing — both nearby and via shuttle to Discovery Basin.

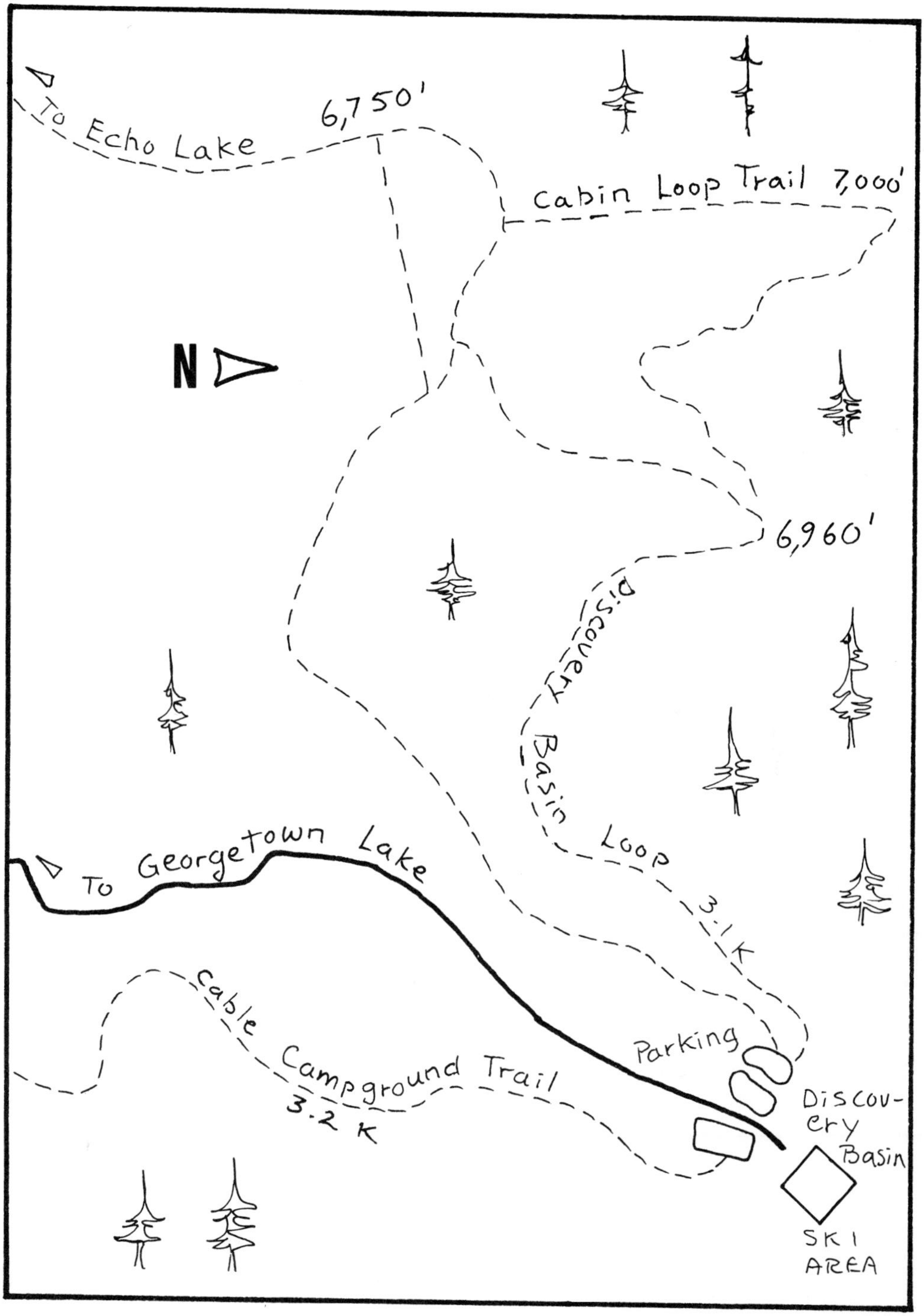

To Echo Lake
6,750'
Cabin Loop Trail 7,000'
N
6,960'
Discovery Basin Loop
3.1 K
To Georgetown Lake
Cable Campground Trail
3.2 K
Parking
Discovery Basin
SKI AREA

Sunshine Health Mines

Location

½ mile east of I-15; take High Ore exit, then frontage road to Berry Meadows Road. 5 miles south of Boulder, Montana; 35 miles south of Helena.

Accommodations

10 units sleep 2 to 7 people each. Total capacity 34. Complete kitchens. Daily rates at $10 for 1; weekly, $130 for 7 people. Camper hookups, available at $6/day or $36/week, include showers and rest rooms.

Services

Nearest services at Boulder.

Trails and Snow Conditions

Ski from cabin door January through March, on unplowed roads at 5,000-foot elevation. Break trail or ski on additional unplowed roads in immediate vicinity. See Boulder Hot Springs listing for designated trails.

Ski Rentals and Lessons

No rentals or lessons.

Reservations

Proprietors need advance notice so they can turn on heat in your cabin. No credit cards. Pets okay.

Sunshine Health Mines
Box E
Boulder, MT 59632
(406) 225-3670

Here's a tidy little hideaway just waiting for discovery by xc skiers. Tucked in sunny Galena Gulch, it is already on the maps of a steady stream of summer guests who seek out the mine for therapeutic purposes.

Visitors who spend time in the underground tunnel claim varying degrees of relief for such ills as arthritis and sinus problems as well as asthma and other respiratory aliments.

Apparently the beneficial effects were first noticed by a woman who accompanied her miner husband on a visit to a Boulder mine. In addition to Sunshine, there are three other health mines in the Boulder/Basin area. It appears that the mines, which traditionally were excavated for gold, silver and lead, give off radon gas during the natural process of decay.

Top: The well-marked entrance to the year around health mine beckons visitors for a treatment. Below: Sturdy cabins in Galena Gulch provide quiet atmosphere, sunny location and virtually unused trails.

Various theories, none with scientific conclusion, account for the healing properties of the gas.

The operators make no claim as to curative powers of the mines, but Boulder visitors have been known to wait their turn for 1½ hours in lines a half mile long. A "treatment" lasts about 1½ hours and the various mines charge $1.50-3 per treatment. Visitors make social gatherings of their pilgrimages and sit in lighted tunnels on comfy chairs — playing cards, piecing together jigsaw puzzles and chatting.

In a Sunshine Mines album of testimonial documents, the letter of one former sufferer reports good results for herself but even more," . . . our dog hasn't had any limping in her leg for months!"

Regardless of your need or inclination for radon gas therapy, you might enjoy a visit to Sunshine's 52-degree cavern after a cold ski outing. Who knows — it may ease those sore muscles!

Mine managers Peggy and Bob Johnson offer cabins which are cheery, warm and well-furnished, right down to toasters, brooms, dust pans and fly swatters.

A delight of a ski tour starts just down the road at the High Ore exit. Drive up the Radon Tunnel road to the Radon turnoff.

The light at the end of the tunnel illuminates what one may expect to find in a health mine — reading material, puzzles, furnishings for tete-a-tete. Mine manager Peggy Johnson demonstrates proper usage of the facility.

Park here, out of traffic's way (the Radon Mine is open year around), and ski up the unplowed road 3 miles to the ghost town of Comet. When you get there, stick to the roads — snow may have blown over old mining holes.

There are some beautiful runs on the way back down. If one person drives the vehicle out, the others can continue skiing the two miles (700 foot elevation drop) from the Radon turnoff back to the interstate.

Another trail option: ski right from your log cabin door up Galena Gulch to Galena Park, about 2½ miles one way. Or continue on the unplowed road, past the park, all the way to Boulder Hot Springs Hotel, about 8 miles, and treat yourself to a dip in one of the hot pools.

The old mining operation at ghost town Comet is within easy ski range along an unused summer vehicle road. In addition to the mining complex, more than 30 buildings, including an old hotel, remain relatively intact.

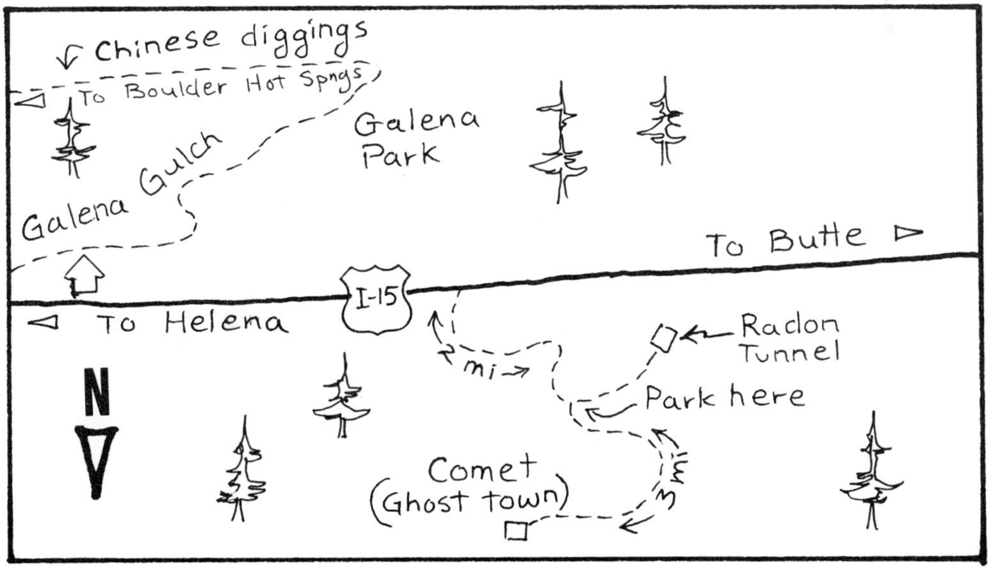

Boulder Hot Springs Hotel

Location
On Montana 69, 2½ miles south of Boulder; 30 miles south of Helena; 35 miles north of Butte.

Accommodations
24 rooms sleep 2-3 people each. Most rooms have ½ baths; showers at pool area. Hotel guests may use hotel kitchen for cooking. Bring towels. Rates, about $24 for two, include use of pools.

Services
Hot pools, beer, wine at hotel. Restaurants, bars, gas and groceries at Boulder.

Trails and Snow Conditions
Skiing at 4,500 feet from hotel door, unless the wind has blown it away. Trails established in Elkhorn Range, 20 miles northeast of the hotel.

Ski Rentals and Lessons
Ski rentals at hotel; no lessons.

Reservations
No credit cards. Management prefers pets be left at home.
Boulder Hot Springs Hotel
P.O. Box 649
Boulder, MT 59632
(406) 225-4272 or 225-9996

Funky people, this is your Xanadu. You won't believe this behemoth of a building when you view it from the highway turn-off, about ¼-mile away. A 1910 article in the *Butte Miner* describes the then-new edifice as "in the style of California Mission architecture."

In those early days it had to be utterly magnificent — a central court with fountain, verandas across the front of the structure. There are hand-painted ceiling borders and intricate wall patterns, a third floor ballroom and finely detailed pillars of Oregon fir in the lobby.

The Butte news item notes that the 125 airy rooms each have "an outside window, electric lights, telephones, hot and cold water." The 13-foot ceiling rooms still accommodate much of the original furniture.

The hotel was heated then, as now, by the hot waters which bubble out of the earth at 180 degrees. The hot springs were discovered in 1871 by one Jim Riley, an unsuccessful and footsore prospector who came down out of the hills and found a hot soak more welcome than gold.

Mountain storms, earthquakes and time have had their way. The grand old palace stands bandaged and splinted, her plaster falling, most of her rooms closed off. Over the years she has been used for various purposes other than guest lodging, her innards have been rearranged, and current owner, Stuart Lewin, is doing well just to keep her open for public use. Despite these problems, available guest rooms are freshly-painted, bright and clean.

Rambling, massive Boulder Hot Springs hotel is an imposing sight from the roadway entry. The old guest resort, famous for its network of indoor and outdoor hot pools, once housed a rest-cure hospital section.

The dungeon-like entry leads you to the wood-heated bar/community kitchen area which is housed in the old rest-cure hospital wing.

The hot springs are the main event. There's a big pool outside and smaller ones, plus steam rooms, inside. On your visit you can join a few regulars in a major source of local entertainment — running across the snow in the middle of the night to jump into the outdoor pool for a hilarious time.

Occasionally there is live music in the decimated old bar room of a Saturday night.

Skiing opportunities in nearby Elkhorn Mountains provide break-your-own trail touring, primarily on unplowed roads. Discover a ghost town or two, enjoy a good downhill return, then come back to the lodge for a soak in a hot pool and a lick in the face by one of three mammoth resident St. Bernards.

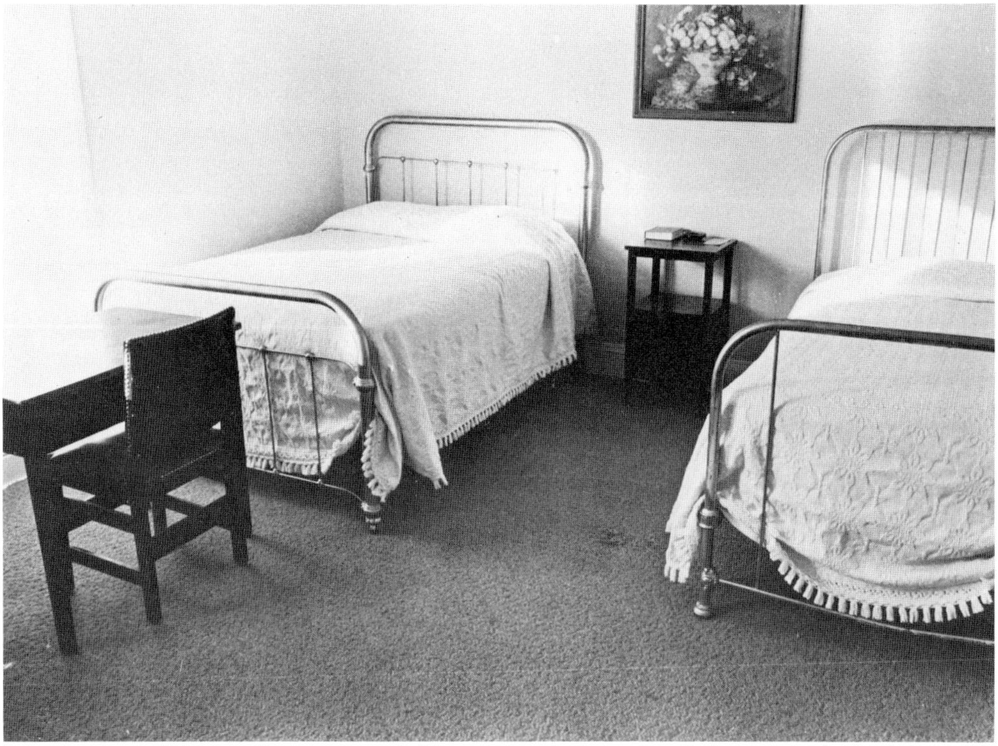

Above: The three guardian St. Bernards at Boulder are as quiet and somber as the building itself. Below: The hot springs hotel is under renovation and newly-remodeled rooms are tidy and bright.

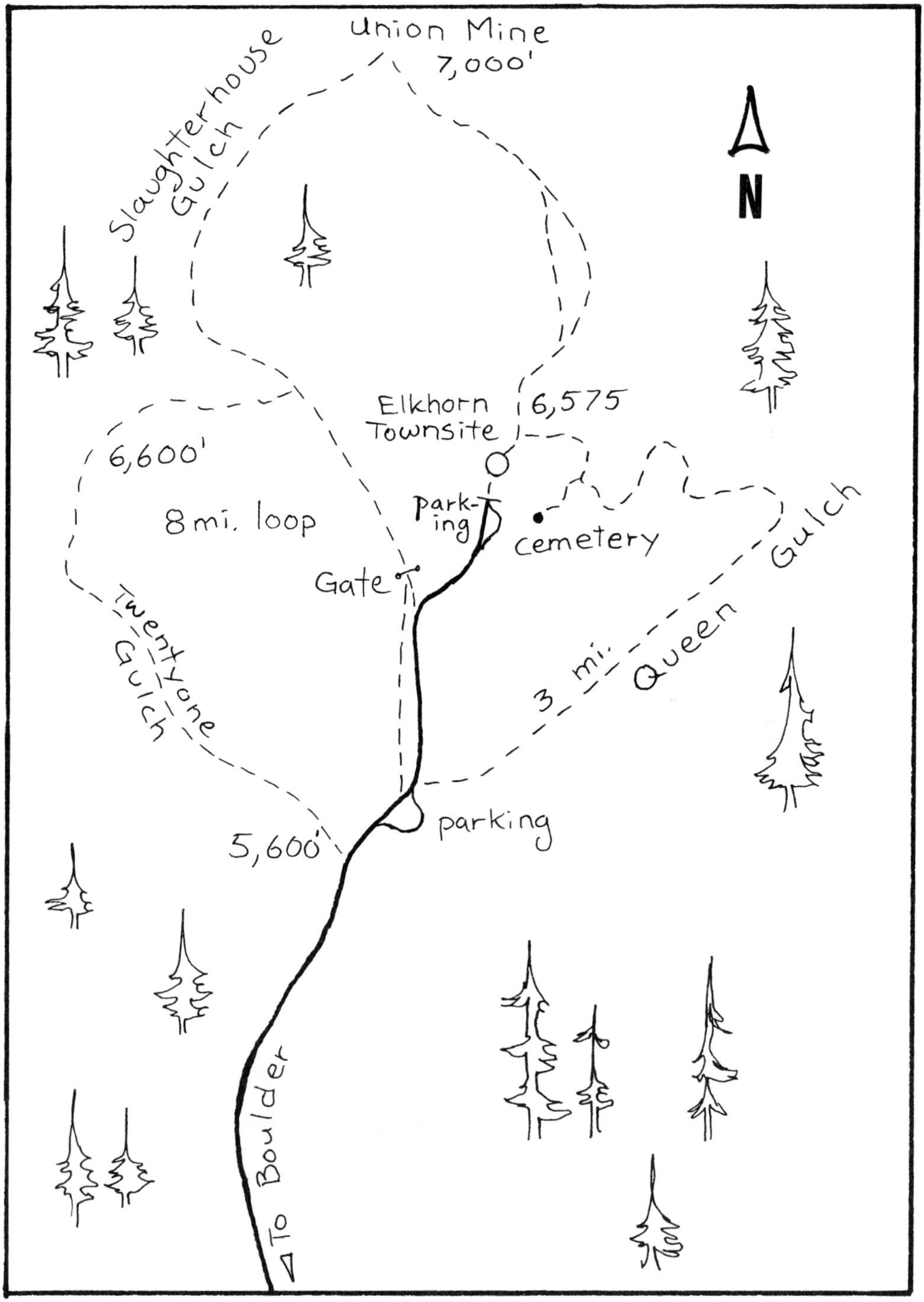
Union Mine
7,000'
N
Slaughterhouse Gulch
Elkhorn Townsite
6,575
6,600'
8 mi. loop
park-ing
cemetery
Gate
Queen Gulch
3 mi.
Twentyone Gulch
parking
5,600'
To Boulder

7 Lazy P Guest Ranch

Location
On Teton Canyon Road, 30 miles northwest of Choteau, Montana; 80 miles northwest of Great Falls.

Accommodations
5 cabins, 3 with kitchens, sleep 4 to 6 people each. Some have fireplaces, all have wood or gas heat. Ranch capacity 25-30 people. $37.50 per night for 4; $6 each extra person.

Services
Restaurant and bar 3 miles. Other services in Choteau.

Trails and Snow Conditions
Skiing on unmarked trails in Lewis and Clark National Forest. Typical trails follow creek beds into canyons and are primarily level. Some steep terrain may be encountered toward Teton Pass. Some skiing on unplowed roads

Ski Rentals and Lessons
No rentals or lessons.

Reservations
Let them know a week in advance so cabins can be heated.
No credit cards.
7 Lazy P Guest Ranch
Box 178
Choteau, MT 59422
(406) 466-2044

The East Front of the Rockies is where the massive mountains and the vast prairie abruptly meet.

The dramatic juncture is where guest ranch operator, Chuck Blixrud, was born. When Chuck was five, his parents moved from their small log house at the mouth of Teton Canyon to a nearby ranch on the flatland. There Chuck was reared. He met and married a local lass whose parents owned the 7 Lazy P, up Teton Canyon, and in 1958, he and Sharon took over operation of the guest ranch.

They have been there ever since, raising two daughters, modernizing log cabins and doing an excellent job of managing a lovely pack outfitting and vacation spot.

Cabins at the 7 Lazy P are everything you'd hope for in a mountain retreat — and more. Except for a roomy new A-frame, all are sturdy, one-story log struc-

Above: Fritz and Ole, friendly resident ski guides at 7 Lazy P, await an opportunity to accompany guests up the trail. Below: The main lodge serves as headquarters for the guest ranch. Accommodations are in cabins.

tures. Though rustic in appearance, cozy interiors of the lodgings are modern, warm, spacious and clean, and floors are carpeted.

The ranch was established in 1930 by a Jack Baker — facilities were primitive then and winter use unheard of. When the Teton Pass downhill ski area opened in 1967, 6 miles beyond the ranch, a plowed road past the 7 Lazy P virtually became guaranteed. Thus the Blixruds were provided with a winter advantage over snowbound guest ranches along the East Front.

Touring choices in Teton Canyon include skiing from your mile-high cabin door up the Middle Fork of the Teton River. The route leads to the famed Bob Marshall Wilderness, 6 miles west.

East of the ranch you can ski on the unplowed road along the South Fork. Beyond the ranch, up Teton Canyon, ski the Jones Creek Trail. Both these tours are primarily level.

From the downhill ski area, continue west along the unplowed road toward Teton Pass to the West Fork — 8 miles round trip. Or take off toward Mt. Lockhart along the North Fork of Waldron Creek for a 4-mile round trip. The pinnacles along the East Front are stunningly beautiful and extremely steep.

Be forewarned that although the creek bed trails generally follow a level course, once they begin their ascent — typically 3 or 4 miles from a trail head — avalanche danger presents too great a risk for ski use. Forest service maps are available at the rangers' offices in Augusta and Choteau.

On a road marker at the mouth of the canyon, author A.B. Guthrie, Jr., poetical-

The guest lounge in the main lodge at 7 Lazy P is used primarily for summer "dudes". But the surroundings are comfortable and there is a supply of reading material and jig saw puzzles. The building houses the owners' home.

ly explains that origins of the Old North Trail near here are "lost in the mists." The prehistoric path is thought to have followed a narrow band of land north/south along the East Front of the Rockies. When ice began to recede from the ice age, ancient peoples migrated south from the Bering Sea and followed the bare land in the shelter of the mountains. Guthrie adds that, "History runs into mystery here." The trail site passes by the cabin where Chuck was born.

In more recent years, old timers still remember hearing "the squeak of the Red River carts." A migration from the Red River area north of the border early in this century brought Canadians to Montana, hauling their belongings in crude, two-wheeled carts. Everything about the carts was wooden including wheels and axles. In order to keep the wood-on-wood from wearing out, huge quantities of axle grease were used, but the carts still squeaked.

During *your* migration to this "undiscovered" country, drive your cart 3 miles east from the ranch to the Cow Track restaurant and lounge. Food is so good here, folks travel 80 miles from Great Falls just to eat dinner. It's open at 3 p.m. Sunday, 5 p.m. Monday through Saturday. You'll need reservations.

This is Charlie Russell country. Images of Ear Mountain and other ridges to the south appear frequently in Russell's famous works. The Russell Gallery and his log cabin studio in Great Falls are open year around and merit a visit.

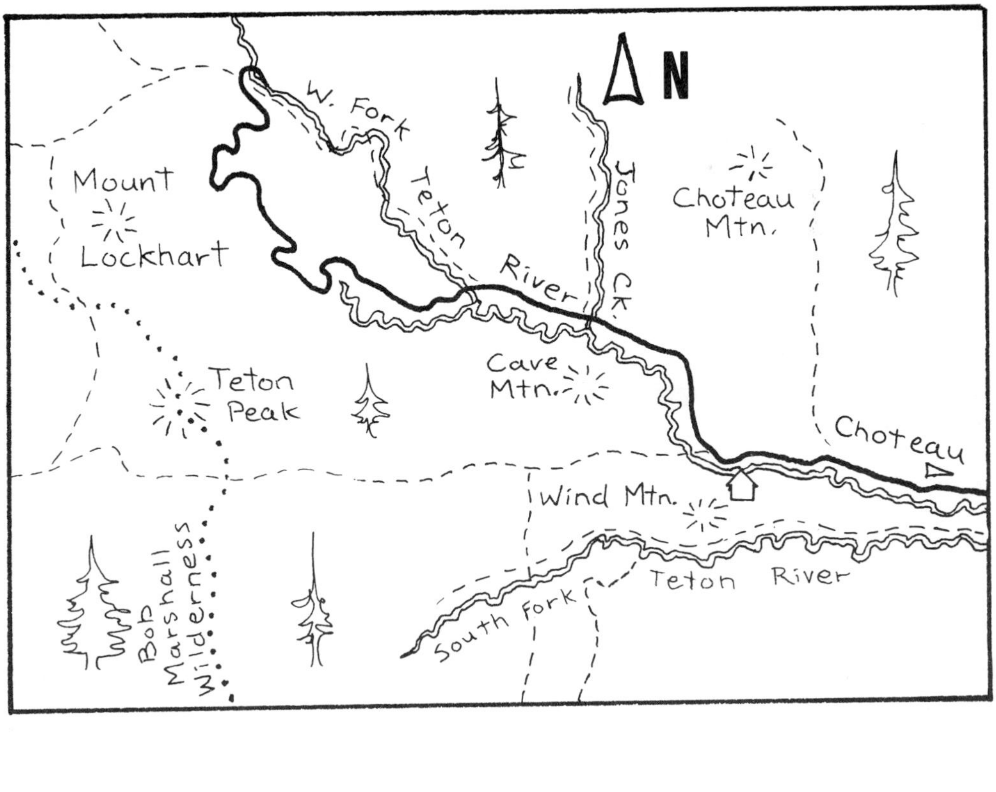

The Poor Farm Sportsman's Lodge

Location
On Sportsman's Lane, off U.S. 89 and 12; 1 mile southwest of White Sulphur Springs, Montana; 100 miles south of Great Falls.

Accommodations
17 lodge rooms accommodate 2-4 people each for a capacity of 36. Bath down hall; no kitchens. $20 single, $25 double, $10/person in "bunk" room. Meal package, $10 per day for breakfast and dinner.

Services
Meals, beer, wine at inn. Restaurant, bars, gas, groceries, hot mineral pools at White Sulphur Springs. 4,800-foot lighted, paved airstrip.

Trails and Snow Conditions
Marked ski trails 30 miles north on U.S. 89 at King's Hill, Divide Road and Jefferson Creek. Additional tour options farther north near Monarch. Ski out the door at the 5,060-foot elevation farm.

Ski Rentals and Lessons
No rentals or lessons.

Reservations
MC, Visa. No pets.
The Poor Farm Sportsman's Lodge
Box 452
White Sulphur Springs, MT 59645
(406) 547-3918

No, the owners aren't suffering from a convoluted sense of humor. This stark-looking, two-story, flatland farm house — a mile out of town — was once a home for the indigent elderly.

Although there is some question as to its original purpose (some think it shady), the sturdy structure was built prior to the turn of the century and was operated for many years as the Meagher (pronounced Mar) County Poor Farm. The 160-acre spread accommodated cows, pigs, chickens, and a garden, and the healthier residents pitched in to help tend the groceries. The days of the Poor Farm ended at the close of World War II and the property has been held in private ownership ever since.

Montana-grown King Wilson purchased the "Farm" in 1979 and opened it as a guest hotel in 1981. That took some extensive renovation and remodeling, King says. So many layers of concrete had been poured in the basement over the years that when King's new furnace was installed, he discovered the equipment was too tall for ceiling clearance. It took a dynamite blast to clear a sufficient-sized hole in the floor to accommodate the standard dimensions of the furnace.

While *Mr.* Wilson is selecting wallpaper and researching 100-year old recipes for the Montana enterprise, *Mrs.* operates the other family business back in Los Angeles. They each like what they're doing.

King's design skills are evident in the tastefully decorated, richly-hued Victorian guest bedrooms. But the modernized bathrooms are the sparkling jewels of the old structure. They are modern, warm and bright, yet retain an old-fashioned

Set on the flatland a mile out of town, the austere exterior appearance of the Poor Farm gives way to lovely and warm ambience inside. The property was operated for years as a county home and opened for guests in 1981.

charm. Most are papered in light blue prints with dazzling fresh white enamel woodwork and immaculate claw-foot bathtubs. The rich oak counter in the Victorian lobby was designed by King.

In the kitchen, guess who is flipping your sourdough pancakes? Right. King presents *good and wholesome* food — like fresh-baked bread made of flour which he grinds from wheat grown on his daddy's Ft. Benton farm. He is one of the more nutritionally-aware people you'll ever meet. Meals are served family-style in the cheery dining room where you might partake of King's made-from-scratch vegetable beef soup and hobo coffee.

Work off your calories by skiing right out the door. But to get into the woods, drive toward Neihart to the Little Belt Mountains, 30 miles north on U.S. 89, past Showdown ski area (downhill). Here you'll find marked trails at King's Hill (no relationship) and Divide Road, both fairly level areas, and popular spots for folks from Great Falls.

There is a *lot* of snowmobile activity nearby and sometimes the machine trails get mixed up with the ski trails, resulting in varying degrees of distraction and confusion. Snow conditions are excellent, however — 25 feet of powder per year — and winter freaks can't stay away. Elevation here is about 7,300 feet.

A few miles north, a parking area is plowed out for ski access to Jefferson Creek, and still farther up the highway, trails head on the road near the community of Monarch. The Lewis and Clark National Forest ranger stations at White

Breakfast and supper may be included in the lodging package at the Poor Farm. The friendly farm provides skier access to the Little Belt Mountains, north of White Sulphur Springs, on the east slope of Montana's Rockies.

Sulphur Springs or at Neihart can help with maps and trail information.

Returning from your day's tour, stop in White Sulphur Springs at the Spa Motel. For $2 you get a towel, a swim suit rental and a soak in the outdoor plunge (89 degrees) or the blistering, but relaxing 110-degree indoor pool.

Merritt Smith, friendly host at the spa, will rent you a room if the Poor Farm is full (or even if it isn't). The Spa has 21 units with phones and TV which rent for $30 per four people. Call Smitty at (406) 547-3366, or write Spa Motel, White Sulphur Springs, MT 59645.

The mineral springs were discovered by, and originally named for, a man called Brewer who built a cabin and settled at the springs. The spa is on a direct route between Ft. Benton (at the end of the steamboat run up the Missouri River from St. Louis) and the gold country between Helena and Idaho. White Sulphur Springs was settled by people who originally came to the area on mining ventures, then metamorphosed into ranchers.

And the railroad, upon which the town's economy was once based, was built by John Ringling of Ringling Brothers Circus fame.

But you can find out all about this, and more, when you end up at the Poor Farm.

Poor Farm owner King Wilson prepares all guest meals at his recently-converted Inn. He designed the interior.

Lone Mountain Ranch

Location
5 miles west of U.S. 191 on Big Sky Road, 45 miles south of Bozeman, Montana; 25 miles north of Yellowstone Park; 50 miles north of West Yellowstone.

Accommodations
40 to 45 guests may be housed in 15 log cabins, all with baths, electric heat and either fireplace or woodstove. No kitchens. Each unit houses 2 to 9 people. Rates, including all meals, start at $338 per person per week (7 nights) or $60 per night — based on 4-persons per cabin.

Services
Dining room, bar, outdoor hot tub, sleigh rides on premises. Groceries, liquor, 3 miles.

Trails and Snow Conditions
35 miles of double machine-set tracks, 25 miles additional marked and unmarked non-maintained trails. All terrain types — flat meadow, woods, creek beds, hillsides — for beginners through experts.

Ski Rentals and Lessons
Complete rentals and equipment, apparel and accessory sales in ski shop. 5 certified ski instructors at guest disposal, included in lodging fee. Wide range of guide services available.

Reservations
By September or October but up to a year in advance for some time slots. AmEx, MC, Visa. Pets discouraged.

Lone Mountain Ranch
Box 145
Big Sky, MT 59716
(406) 995-4644

"Cross country skiing is just *not* a herd sport in my book," proclaims Bob Schaap, papa of Lone Mountain Ranch — a name that should be synonomous with the utmost superlative in a xc ski center.

Bob and spouse Vivian own 400 acres adjacent to Big Sky downhill resort area and in addition, they lease about 2,000 acres of national forest lands. But even with all that room for expansion, they intend to maintain the facility at its present capacity in order to uphold the excellent quality program currently being offered.

At Lone Mountain, the entire staff is considered family, and they really take care of you. Instructors are there if you want them — or if you don't — to guide you in your very first attempt on skis or just to file down a few rough edges. Or teach you telemarking.

The chef will blow your diet and your mind all at the same time. Former Twin Cities (Minnesota) Big Time, he seems driven to outdoing himself day upon day.

Lone Mountain Ranch offers virtually everything to the ski tourer — miles of set tracks, access to the wilderness and Yellowstone Park, full-time ski instruction, gourmet meals and a lovely setting.

The weekly "on the snow" ski tour luncheon alone is worth the entire trip to Lone Mountain, no matter how far you have to drive. Think about a crackling wood fire; delicately seasoned roast beef sliced on-site; salmon with mustard/dill sauce; breaded veal strips with bearnaise sauce; an intricately-carved watermelon boat, complete with buxom figurehead; a mini-keg of beer; two kinds of wine and three desserts — one of them chocolate mousse!

Pampered doesn't even come close to describing how you'll feel.

All of the build-up is not for naught. You are in for a really great time at Lone Mountain — if you can book space. Most guests are return customers who stay a week, then reserve for the following year before their departure.

Bob's commitment to his goal of "having the best Nordic center in the country" is reflected partly in the ranch xc grooming equipment which he believes to be the most sophisticated in the Northwest. At a $24,000 price tag, he is probably correct. A Bombi (small Bombardier snow cat) is used to tow a combination ice breaker and packer and a double track setter. Trails, which were engineered by Bob, are groomed almost continuously along a swath 8+ feet wide.

At the Horsefly Saloon (the former tack room in a building which was once a sod-roofed barn), Conrad will prepare you a frothy hot-buttered rum made from the toothsome ice cream recipe. While you're at the Horsefly, be aware that the bar horn may be sounded for listed reasons, among them . . . "to discourage the use of college words" and "to recognize tips."

Each ranch-style cabin at Lone Mountain is immaculately maintained and gracious enough to be a home away from home. Log interiors and wood fires round out the inviting atmosphere.

During your stay at Lone Mountain, if you should possibly tire of the delightful, and some very challenging trails on the premises, here are a few more options:

— Guided naturalist trips to Yellowstone Park, three times a week. Groups of no more than seven people will learn of trees, animals and geology of the Park on an all-day tour. Cost to ranch guests is $16, including lunch.

— Spanish Peaks Wilderness tours — great for telemarkers — $12.

— A special treat is a back-country overnight to a cabin about 7 miles one way. Cost for a group of five, $125 including all meals.

If you're still looking for diversion, go on up to Big Sky, 5 miles west, and rub Gore-tex with the downhillers at this posh and complete resort.

At Lone Mountain, evening programs in the "barn" lounge will provide information on winter survival as well as naturalist topics. Plenty of help abounds — the bulletin board in the ski shop greets you with avalanche conditions and wax of the day.

The weekly on-the-snow lunch feast at Lone Mountain is a bountiful reward for vigorous trail exertion.

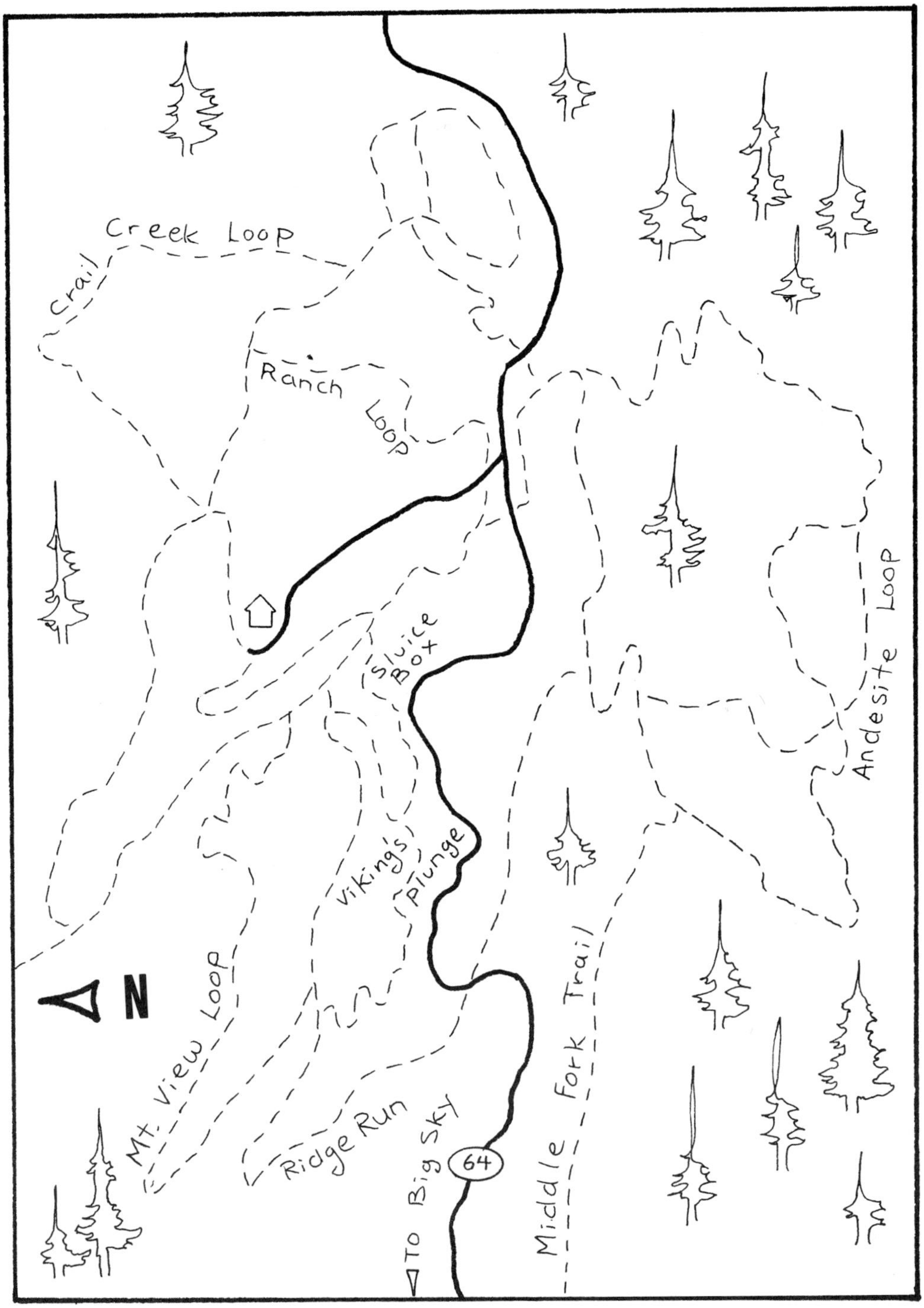
Crail Creek Loop
Ranch Loop
Sluice Box
Viking's Plunge
Mt. View Loop
Ridge Run
To Big Sky
64
Middle Fork Trail
Andesite Loop
N

Bridger Mountain Lodge

Location
1 mile off U.S. 86, 16 miles northeast of Bozeman, Montana; ¼ mile from Bridger Bowl downhill ski area.

Accommodations
7 motel units and 2 cabins, each with 2 double beds, some with hideabeds. Private baths; no kitchens. Rates, starting at $18.50 per person per night (4 to a room, 3-night package), include breakfast and dinner.

Services
Food, sauna on premises. Fast food, bar, live music on weekends at Flaming Arrow Ski Touring Centre "Pub", 1 mile. Restaurant, lounges at Bridger Bowl. Other services in Bozeman. Airport pick-up at Bozeman.

Trails and Snow Conditions
15-20 kilometers machine-set double tracks at Flaming Arrow Ski Touring Centre maintained daily, or as needed. All trails are marked. Touring on a variety of terrain for every ability level. $2 trail use fee.

Ski Rentals and Lessons
Certified ski school with 9 instructors. Complete rental service.

Reservations
Reservation requirements vary, but at least one day's notice is needed. No credit cards. Pets discouraged and not permitted on trails.

Bridger Mountain Lodge
Box 374
Bozeman, MT 59715
(406) 587-3088

Visit Flaming Arrow Ski Touring Centre for a xc lesson and be prepared for almost anything. Your instructor may show up in fake nose and mustache, Jimmy Buffett togs or who-knows-what zany outfit.

The three loony proprietors of Flaming Arrow — Tony Forrest, John Kravetz and Larry Wilson — have a no-nonsense policy regarding the operation of their popular touring area. It is, "to make skiing fun for us. If we have a good time so does everyone else". When the humor begins to pall for one of their instructors — a sort of burn-out — they "fire 'em!"

Don't let all the slapstick fool you. Instruction at Flaming Arrow is top quality. Both Larry and Tony are PSIA instruction examiners for the Northern Rocky Mountain Division and are on the Nordic demonstration team.

The entrepreneurs are also "working managers" who participate in such hefty events as the annual Wisconsin Berkenbeiner (surviving the 7,000-competitor mass start is a major feat).

The trio is going into its fourth year of proprietorship at Flaming Arrow, also known as FAST. They lease the building and land from Bridger Mountain Lodge owners. Trails have been designed and

Top: Larry Wilson and Tony Forrest, partners in a Montana Nordic program, are natural hams. Below: Bridger Canyon's Flaming Arrow Ski Touring Centre offers fun and an extensive xc trail system.

copiously labled with such landmarks as "Lawrence Elk", "Dr. J's Maze" and "Nirvana Meadows." The trail map provides sufficient reading material to take up a coffee break, while supplying excellent information.

One of the more notable features (of many notable features) at FAST is the frequency and variety of scheduled events. Something is planned for almost every weekend — winter skills and telemark clinics, kids' programs, races (*always* in costume) and daily Montana State University physical education classes.

Back at your cabin, enjoy a warmer-upper in the sauna. Betsy Taylor, manager of the lodge, will have snacks ready in the rustic and beautiful fireplace room. Guests make themselves at home here, and as Betsy says, people "come as guests, but leave as friends."

Dinner is a comfortable, family-style affair with hearty homemade fare which Betsy prepares and serves with pride.

Motel rooms are spacious and adequately-furnished. Cabins, while older and smaller, are clean and comfortable.

History of the 600-acre ranch is colorful. The first structure was a cabin built in 1878 which served as officers' quarters at a military sawmill. Ranch founder Evans Forsythe and his spunky bride Jane bought the property in 1931. In order that co-ed Jane not lose her Vassar scholarship, their marriage had remained unannounced for two years. Upon their arrival at the cabin, they found that the floor had been eaten away by porcupines. Unflapped, they began building the "Forsythe Range" — a ranch for dudes. Later owners changed the name to Bridger Mountain Guest Ranch. The Bridger Canyon spread is at 6,000 feet elevation.

This area is a good choice for those seeking a busy, active touring center and the kind of snow locals refer to as "cold smoke."

Accommodations at Bridger Mountain Lodge are available in motel-type units or small log cabins. Guests enjoy home-style meals in the main lodge. Flaming Arrow ski trails may be accessed at cabin door.

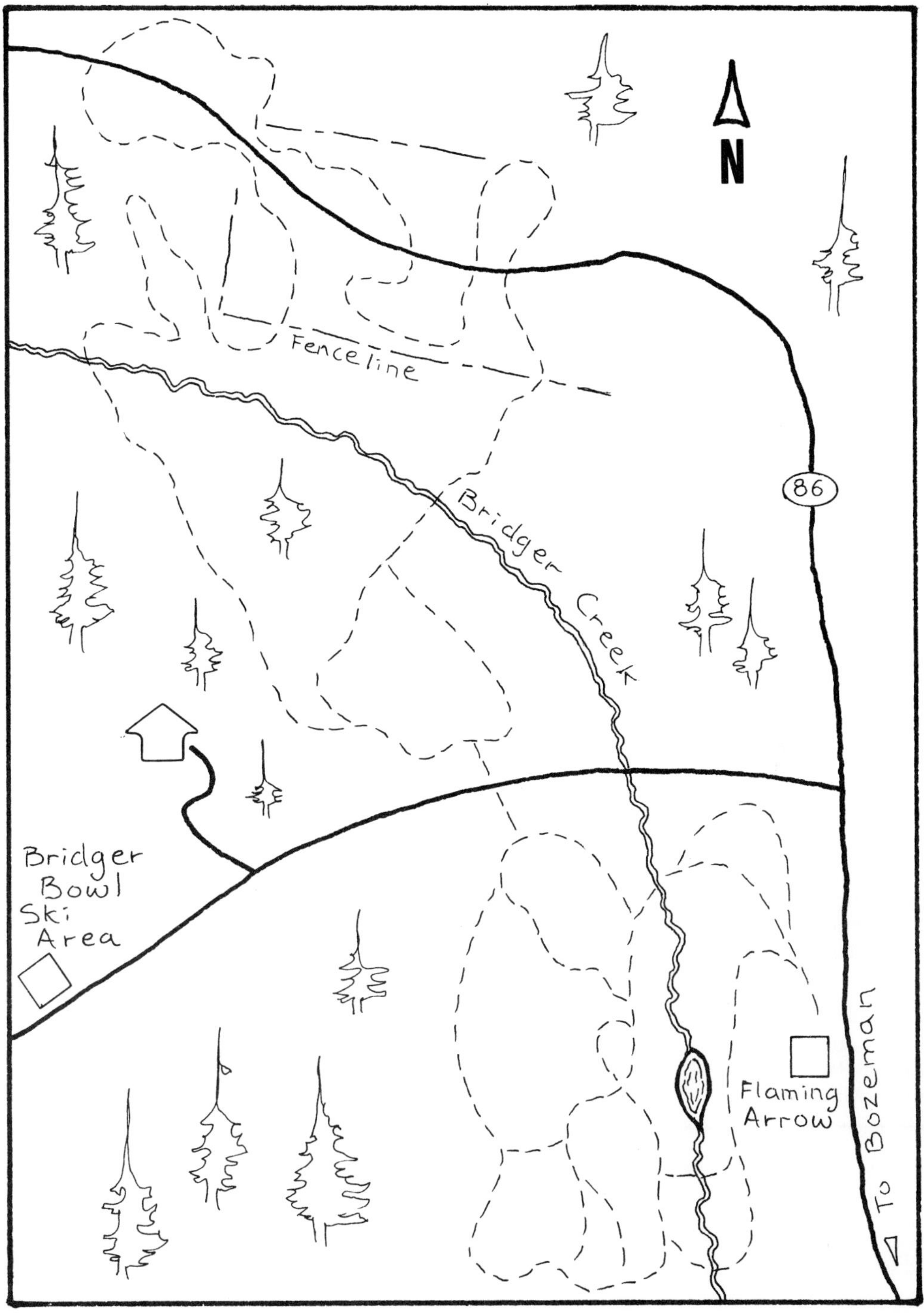
N
Fenceline
Bridger Creek
86
Bridger
Bowl
Ski
Area
Flaming
Arrow
To Bozeman

Chico Hot Springs

Location

3 miles east of U.S. 89; 26 miles south of Livingston, Montana; 31 miles north of entrance to Yellowstone National Park.

Accommodations

60 lodge rooms, with and without private baths; 11 motel units, none with kitchens. 3 fully-contained houses (1 log, 2 chalets) sleep 4, 6 and 10 people. Houses have kitchens, washers, dryers, fireplaces. Resort capacity 130. Convention facilities for 300. Rates range from $24 for a double in the lodge to $110 per night for a 2-bedroom chalet.

Services

Dining room, snack bar, saloon, hot pools at resort. Gas and groceries, 3 miles.

Trails and Snow Conditions

1 mile to nearest trail head. 15 miles to extensive trail system on national forest land. Many marked trails as well as unlimited touring in Yellowstone Park. Excellent snow conditions at Cooke City, 55 miles east of Gardiner. Information available at forest service office in Livingston and Mammoth Hot Springs Park Headquarters, at Park entrance.

Ski Rentals and Lessons

Crazy Mountain Sports ski shop on premises. Extensive rentals. XC equipment, apparel and accessories for sale. Certified instructors available for all ability levels with teaching emphasis on trail experience. Guided Tours, $35 locally or $40 into the Park, include trail lunch.

Reservations

Reservations suggested always. MC, Visa.
Chico Hot Springs
Pray, MT 59065
(406) 333-4411

Mention Chico Hot Springs to folks in Montana (or anywhere else, for that matter) and you'll be told, "Be sure to go there. They have the best restaurant in the state."

Indeed it is imaginative and well-prepared food. Breakfast eggs are delicately scrambled and coffee couldn't be better. On Sundays, you can partake of a buffet.

Dinner selections range from basic steak or beef burger to Crown Roast of Lamb and Roast Duckling au Grand Marnier. There is a fine choice of seafood, including a sole and King Crab dish baked in a fish-shaped, glazed pastry crust which appears like a whole fish resting upon your plate.

The hotel was opened in 1900, at the advent of large-scale, destination spas. The early-day resort housed a hospital where patients were treated by resident physicians. Railcars carried passengers up Paradise Valley where they disembarked at the settlement of Emigrant, three miles from Chico. Here they were fetched by classy horse-drawn "wagonette' (leather seats, glass windows), and transported to the spa.

In 1902 an indoor pool was installed. You can still swim in it, but it's now an *outdoor* plunge — in 1957 the roof fell in. A smaller, and hotter, open-air pool is under shelter. Both pools are free to hotel guests. Enclosed "hot pots" are available at $5 per couple.

Upon entering the lobby, you will be greeted by a sign which proclaims, "The management of Chico Hot Springs reserves the right to refuse service to anyone not in a good mood."

It's difficult to imagine any gloom here — Chico is a place for relaxing.

The spacious grounds at Chico Hot Springs Resort encompass the lofty lodge complex, motel units, three separate guest houses, an old stone barn and the new Nordic ski shop, which is housed in the former carriage house.

It's also a place for skiing. At nearby Emigrant Gulch, named for 11,000-foot Emigrant Peak behind the lodge, novices can stretch their muscles. Ski one mile to mining camp White City where one prospector still tunnels for gold. More advanced skiers can follow the unplowed road another eight miles up a rolling hill ascent. Mill Creek drainage, 15 miles southeast of Chico, is a popular touring area and provides thrills for all ability levels.

Wildlife lovers, head south into the Park. Drive east from Mammoth toward Cooke City and you'll practically need a tank to get through the ubiquitous herds of elk and bison. Along the way are a myriad of trail heads, most of which are identified on maps available at the Park Visitors' Center. Select from summer trails and unplowed roads or take off through the open country on exploration adventures at about 6,200 feet elevation.

It's a long way to Cooke City from Chico — 85 miles — but snow conditions are so fine that many Chico guests opt to stay there at least one night. The few winter residents of Cooke City keep three motels open — All Seasons Inn, Mus' Rest Motel and Hoosiers' Motel. They may be contacted at Cooke City, MT 59020.

Ma Perkins Cafe, the Elkhorn Saloon, and dining and drink facilities at the All Seasons are also open and bustling. Gas, limited groceries and a post office round out Cooke City's winter services.

This area is just starting to be discovered by xc types. The snow at 7,651 feet is

Chico offers guests three floors of lodging, a complex of natural hot water pools, bar, excellent dining, and the fascinating history of a turn of the century luxury spa. The busy resort is popular year around.

fantastic and a fresh dusting falls almost every morning. It's Snowmobile City, however, and organized rallies are scheduled almost every weekend.

Fortunately, wilderness areas are off-limits to machines, and there's one on each side of Cooke City. The Beartooth-Absaroka Wilderness is 5 miles north on a snowmachine-packed road. The ascent is steep for the first 2 miles or so and then levels off. To the south, the wilderness can be accessed via Irma Mine, only 1½ miles from town. From here you can ski around extinct volcano Republic Mountain.

Bear in mind that xc experience, skills and proper equipment are your ticket to safe passage along most of these mountainous, heavy-snow routes. Avalanche danger is common and your path must be chosen with care and informed awareness.

You can still have a good time touring closer in on the packed roads near town and up the unplowed highway to Colter Pass. Snow is excellent here, even when it is melting or gone in the Park.

Cooke City, originally named Shoofly, was settled as a gold, silver and lead mining town more than a century ago. During the period 1908-09, the mines were worked primarily by people from the Finnish community of Red Lodge, 64 miles to the east by modern day road. Each weekend the Red Lodge Finns would ski home and then back again to the mines for work on Monday morning. Nowadays, the Cooke City-Red Lodge highway, over 11,000-foot Beartooth Pass is plowed June 15 to October 15 only.

Back at Chico, stop by the "Old Saloon" (Est. 1902) at Emigrant Junction for a true taste of Montana. Cowpokes — the real item, folks — saunter in, still sheathed in chaps after a hard day on the range. Take a look at the hitching rail on your way out. Very likely a cow pony or two will be tied there.

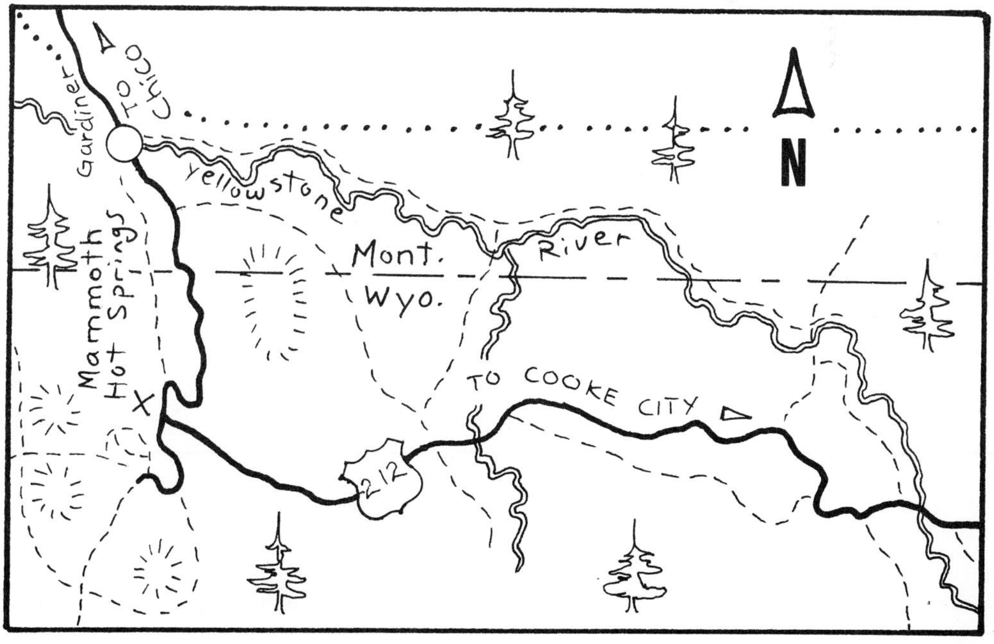

Burnt Leather Ranch

Location
On West Boulder Road, 2½ miles west of McLeod, Montana; 26 miles east of Livingston; 18 miles southwest of Big Timber.

Accommodations
Duplex cabins house a maximum of 8 guests. Cabins are primitive — no electricity, indoor plumbing or kitchens. Light is by gas lantern; structures are insulated and wood-heated. Although bedding is provided, bring a sleeping bag for cold Montana nights. $85 per day per person includes all meals, instruction/guide services and transportation via mule sleigh, 6-17 miles from main ranch to ski camp.

Services
Meals provided, sauna. All other services at Livingston or Big Timber.

Trails and Snow Conditions
20 miles of marked trails, some machine-packed. Selection includes groomed ski routes as well as summer trails. Terrain varieties for all ability levels. Elevation 5,600 feet.

Ski Rentals and Lessons
Ski instruction, guides provided.

Reservations
Give them a few days' notice so they can haul in supplies.
No credit cards. Pets "not a problem".
Burnt Leather Ranch
McLeod, MT 59052
(406) 932-2412

"If you want square dancing every Tuesday at 2 in the afternoon, this isn't the place you're looking for."

So says Sharon Reid who, with her husband Chuck, operates West Boulder cattle operation, Burnt Leather Ranch.

Sharon and Chuck tailor-make winter tours for xc skiers on their summer guest ranch quarters. But the program is not a scheduled, social and recreational routine. The ranch is isolated and every trip is different, ordered around the personalities of the guests. That's why the Reids keep it small.

When you arrive at the ranch, you're as likely as not to find Chuck and/or Sharon tending the mules. They have 30 head of the colorful critters and use them primarily for summer and fall pack trips. In winter, the hard-working, intelligent beasts, with such catchy names as 'Mon Back and Doo Dah, are busy hauling hay . . and guests. Panhandler Debbie, 17 hands tall, will try to mooch any choice tidbit you might bring her way.

Life is fairly simple at the ranch. Chuck and Sharon's Burnt Leather, where they live and where the real work goes on, it's accessible by vehicle year around. But the "play area" where guests stay, called the upper ranch, is reached over winter snows by mule sled.

The ranch has been in Chuck's family since the mid-30's. The Reids added to the guest ranch and hunting trip business in 1980 by opening skier facilities in winter.

The main ranch at Burnt Leather, a working cattle operation, is accessible by vehicle year around. Winter guests are transported several miles by mule sled to ski cabin accommodations at the "upper ranch."

Says Sharon, of the guest component, "We're doing something we like to do or we wouldn't be doing it. The cattle business is the pits! The people are what make it fun for us."

Burnt Leather philosophy toward guest/staff relationships is to rotate the duties of full-time employes so they don't suffer from burn-out by permanent responsibility for and continuous contact with guests. Special guides are brought in for winter ski touring and lessons. Robin and Paul Dix of Livingston accompany the Reids and guests to the upper ranch on an "on-call" basis. Fun for them, fun for the skiers. Paul is a photographer and the pair provides custom instruction and guide services.

An example of one of your tour options while visiting Burnt Leather is an overnight (or longer) tour from the upper ranch to Mission Camp, six miles on a packed trail. This area was originally settled as a homestead, while the upper ranch is a former tie camp, where timber for railroad ties was cut and hand hewn.

The upper camps border on the Absaroka-Beartooth Wilderness Area. The territory is rich in mineral deposits and would have been geologically explored by now were it not for its wilderness status. Local residents credit the conservation effort and success to the late U.S. Senator, Mike Mansfield. The Montana lawmaker served his state long and well, and the Absaroka-Beartooth was established as a tribute after his death.

The region has an interesting history. Cattle ranching in Montana began here. In 1867, 1,600 head of beef were driven from Texas to range in the Livingston/Boulder area. This territory was chosen because of the frequency of Chinook winds which take off the winter chill.

Left: Chuck Reid, Burnt Leather proprietor, utilizes team effort on the ranch. Right: Moocher Debbie clears the fence line of all paddock-mates so that she has full attention of visitors bearing tasty morsels.

"Burnt Leather" has a bit of history of its own. A former owner, a cowpoke who fancied himself a poet, used the title to describe what happens when a branding iron meets cow hide.

When Sharon isn't doing ranch chores, such as repairing harness, she's shuttling the two children back and forth to school in Livingston — a four-hour daily commute.

Busy hands are happy hands and, according to Sharon, "If you're not doing what you like, you're not going to be good at it."

The 85% repeat business by Burnt Leather guests is an indicator that Chuck and Sharon are good at what they do.

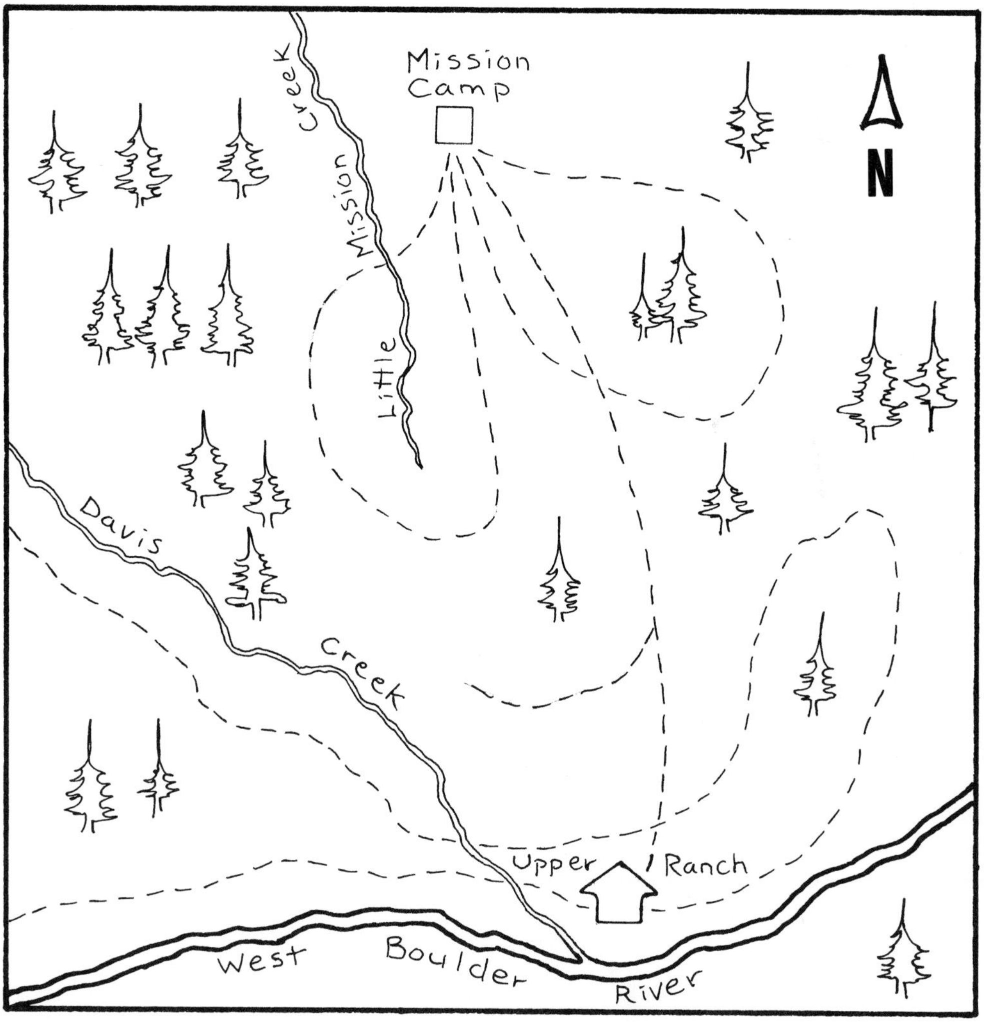

Hawley Mountain Guest Ranch

Location
44 miles south of Big Timber on Main Boulder Road (Highway 298); 74 miles southeast of Livingston, Montana; 125 miles southwest of Billings; 28 miles north of Yellowstone Park. *Ski in 6-12 miles or be transported by snowmobile.*

Accommodations
4 units in main lodge building (with separate outside entrances) sleep 4 people each in beds — 1 double, 2 bunks. Sleeping bags on floor okay. Bathroom downstairs; no shower in winter. Each unit has kitchenette. Bring towels. $30 per day per person includes all meals, fireside wine party.

Services
Family-style meals served at lodge. Post office and public phone at McLeod, approximately 30 miles north. All other services in Big Timber.

Trails and Snow Conditions
Miles of skiing on summer horse trails, unplowed roads and creek drainage. Some trails machine-packed. Terrain primarily rugged, although novices will find ample meadow and riverside touring areas.

Ski Rentals and Lessons
No rentals or lessons.

Reservations
Let them know in advance. No credit cards. Pets okay.
Hawley Mountain Guest Ranch
Box 4
McLeod, MT 59052
(409) 932-2723 (message phone)

The Eagles Nest Lodge at Hawley Mountain Guest Ranch is literally a breathtaking sight for the unprepared. As you round a bend in the road along the canyon floor, suddenly there appears to the watchful a gabled log lodge, perched 200 feet straight up, on the edge of a rock cliff.

The spiky mountains surrounding the 156-acre ranch form a wild and beautiful setting for the impressive structure.

Bill and Sadako Jarrett built the lodge after they came to operate the summer guest ranch in 1970. Bill comes by it naturally — his granddaddy bought the property 70 years ago. Bill has been a pack outfitter for 19 years. He and Sadako opened the ranch for winter use seven years ago.

Nature has been left intact at Eagles Nest. A cliff-top rock formation protrudes through the floor of the common room. A massive round central fireplace is constructed of local rock and is glass-enclosed. The circular hearth is set with river rock which had to be dug out of ice at the time of construction!

Life couldn't be much more laid back around Bill and Sadako. Anyone would feel comfortable here, but it's an especially good choice for groups. Pick up your plate at mealtime from the bar at the tiny kitchen and join the rest of the folks at the long family-style table. Gaze

Cliff-top Eagles Nest Lodge presides over Hawley Mountain Guest Ranch from its lofty throne-like perch. The ranch rests in a narrow valley miles off the beaten track and is accessed in winter via skis or snow machine.

through picture windows across the narrow valley at double-peaked, 10,148-foot Mt. Hawley as you munch.

Your breakfast very well might include a whopper of a Rainbow trout, *fresh*-caught by Bill earlier in the morning through the ice on the ranch pond.

Ancient and not-so-ancient inhabitants have made their mark on the area. More than 7,000 years ago, early man left stone tools on old river terraces. They were excavated in a 1971 archeological dig on the Jarrett property by Montana State University students and faculty. Evidence of six prehistoric cultures was uncovered in the dig.

A few thousand years later, around 1870, gold was discovered in the canyon and then the good times started to roll. Independence, 14 miles south at the end of the road, had a heyday from about 1878 to 1893. During the early days of the lusty town virtually *all* community services were provided except education and religon.

Bill will transport you to now-ghosted 10,000-foot Independence via snowmobile, and you can ski back to Eagles Nest — downhill all the way. It's a 14-mile, 4,000-foot elevation drop on a snow-packed road. Or if you like, he'll drop you off at an overnight cabin and you can ski back next day on either of two routes. One is the road you came in on, the other forks east and eventually circles Hawley Mountain back to the ranch. Both are approximately 14 miles in length and should be attempted only by experienced skiers.

If you're up for it, Bill will guide you just about as far as it's humanly possible to go. A 20-mile day trip to Cooke City or Yellowstone Park, through the Absaroka-Beartooth Wilderness, is one possibility. For the hardy, it ends with a 9-mile uphill.

Bill is definitely of the hardy rank. He relates a story of a 45-mile trek by snowshoe which started one morning at eight and ended about midnight. He recommends "three essentials" for such esca-

Part of the rock cliff upon which Eagles Nest reposes juts through the floor in the spacious main room of the lodge. The view from the cliff edge is of meadow elk and double-summit Mt. Hawley.

pades: sandwiches, a flashlight and a bottle of aspirin, the latter "so you can keep going no matter how it hurts."

Bill, who augments his winter ranch duties by doing snow survey work, states that winter is his favorite time. There are "no crowds, no mosquitos, no water snakes."

Be aware that Hawley Mountain Ranch is a retreat for skiers and "sledders" (as snowmobilers are called in Big Timber) alike. Somehow, though, it all works out. The two groups seldom share the same weekend. Even when they do, this breed of machiners is different. Instead of buzzing around in circles and figure-eights they go off on destination tours, just like you do. And remember — it's a snowmachine that packs your trails and makes it easier for you to get to Eagles Nest.

Travel tip: pack *light* if you're going in by snowmobile. There is room on the machine for your skis, but not much else. Try to cram everything into a day pack.

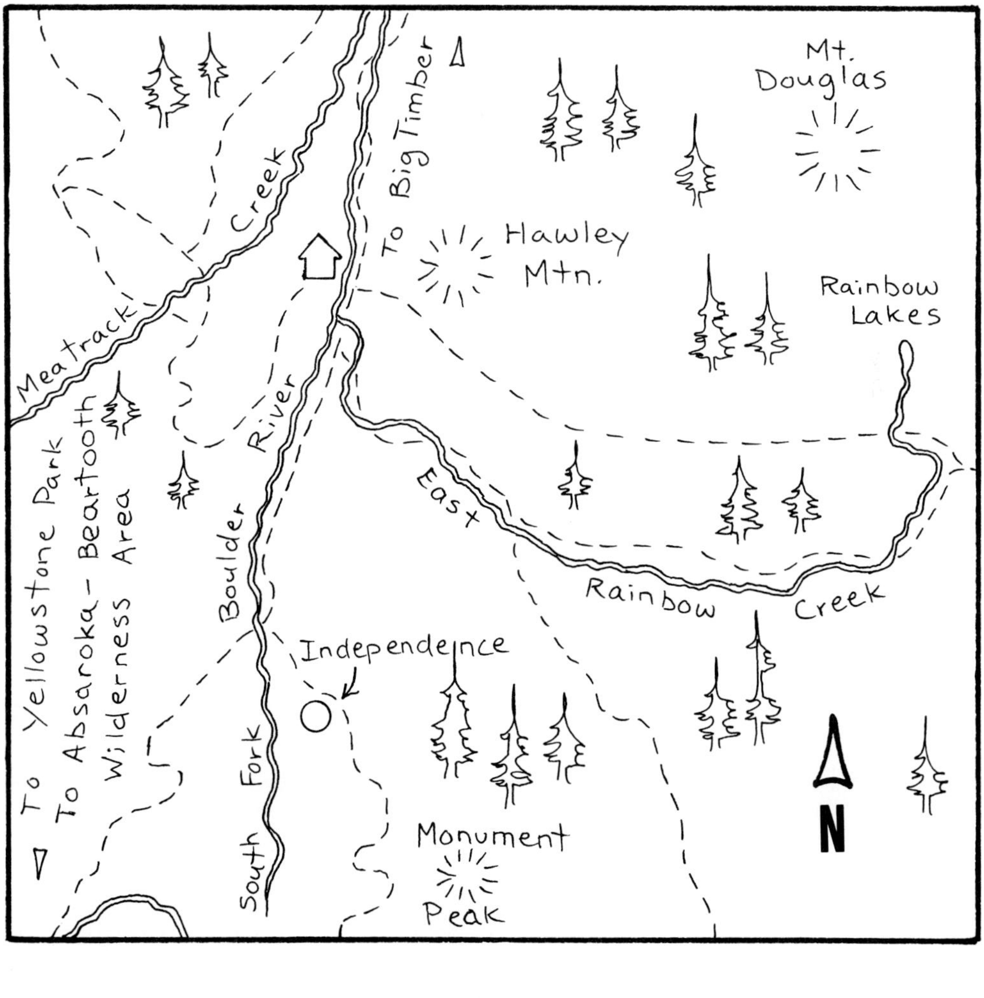

Wyoming

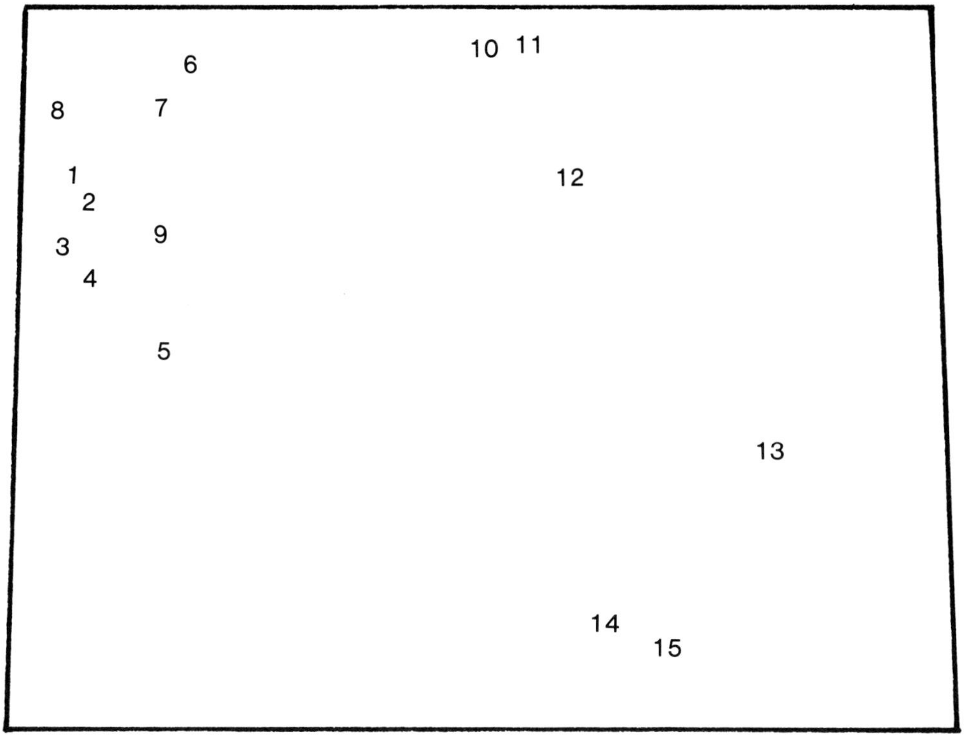

1 Flagg Ranch
2 Triangle X Ranch
3 Western Motel
4 Camp Creek Inn
5 White Pine Lodge
6 Rawhide Ranch
7 Pahaska Tepee
8 Old Faithful Snow Lodge
9 Wind River Ranch
10 Bear Lodge
11 Arrowhead Lodge
12 Meadowlark Lake Lodge
13 Esterbrook Lodge
14 Hotel Wolf
15 Medicine Bow Lodge

Flagg Ranch

Location
On U.S. 89 and 287, 2 miles south of Yellowstone Park; 23 miles north of Moran Junction, Wyoming; 55 miles north of Jackson. *Winter access from south only.*

Accommodations
54 new, modern motel units sleep 1 to 5 people each. No kitchens. Rates: 1 or 2, $48; 3 or 4, $52. Inquire about special January packages.

Services
Dining room, snack bar, saloon, groceries, gifts, package liquor, gas on premises.

Trails and Snow Conditions
Unmarked, non-maintained trails adjacent to lodge area. Fairly flat touring, in and out of trees. Share some with snowmobiles. 6,886 feet elevation.

Ski Rentals and Lessons
Rentals on premises. Lessons available by advance arrangement.

Reservations
3 to 4 weeks for holidays. MC, Visa. Pets okay.
Flagg Ranch
P.O. Box 187
Moran, WY 83013
(307) 733-8761 in-state
(800) 443-2311, toll-free from out of state

It may not be a real ranch — it's actually a spiffily-done highway tourist accommodation tucked in between Yellowstone and Grand Teton National Parks — but it offers snazzy lodging, a short ski-hop to a natural hot springs, direct access to both parks and more snow than you can shake a shovel at.

Deluxe warm-toned guest rooms are attractive and tastefully decorated.

Ski trails at Flagg are not marked but resort employees are out there on the boards every day. Decide on your destination, then follow their tracks.

There are three basic tour choices: 1) Go north up the Snake River, east of the highway, to Yellowstone Park — it's about 4 miles round trip. 2) A heavy-duty skier might select Grassy Lake Road, 18 miles round trip. Ski southwest from the lodge. 3) Or, most popular, the Huckleberry Hot Springs tour — 3 miles round trip from the lodge or 6 miles round trip from the road. A natural ex-

New accommodations at Flagg Ranch offer attractive surroundings to northwest Wyoming visitors. The lodge complex is adjacent to the major highway connecting Yellowstone and Grand Teton National Parks.

perience in three natural hot pools. Trail delights include the possibility of sighting trumpeter swans, moose and Canada geese.

Unlike the West Yellowstone entrance, the south Park gate area is relatively calm in the snowmobile category, and snow machines don't use the area west of the highway. In both Yellowstone and Teton, over-the-snow vehicles are restricted to designated roads. You will find a few snowmobilers at Flagg Ranch, but many of them head on into Yellowstone Park.

Twelve-passenger snow coach transportation to Old Faithful via the nearby south Park entrance departs from Flagg Ranch. Cost is $47.84 round trip, including tax. A special treat would be to combine your stay at Flagg with an overnight or two in the Park at Snow Lodge (see separate listing).

The resort, owned by International Leisure Hosts, lost its main lodge to fire in March 1981. In the interim, until a replacement is built, various services — office, dining room, bar — are housed in separate log structures. The temporary buildings once served as guest cabins and have been moved to a central location near the highway.

The Burnt Bear Saloon was named for the scorched, carved-wood bear salvaged from the old lodge. The relic now resides behind the new bar.

Wapiti elk are a common winter sight to Yellowstone Park visitors. The snow coach to Old Faithful and geyser basins area departs from Flagg Ranch daily and many guests opt to stay a night or two in the Park.

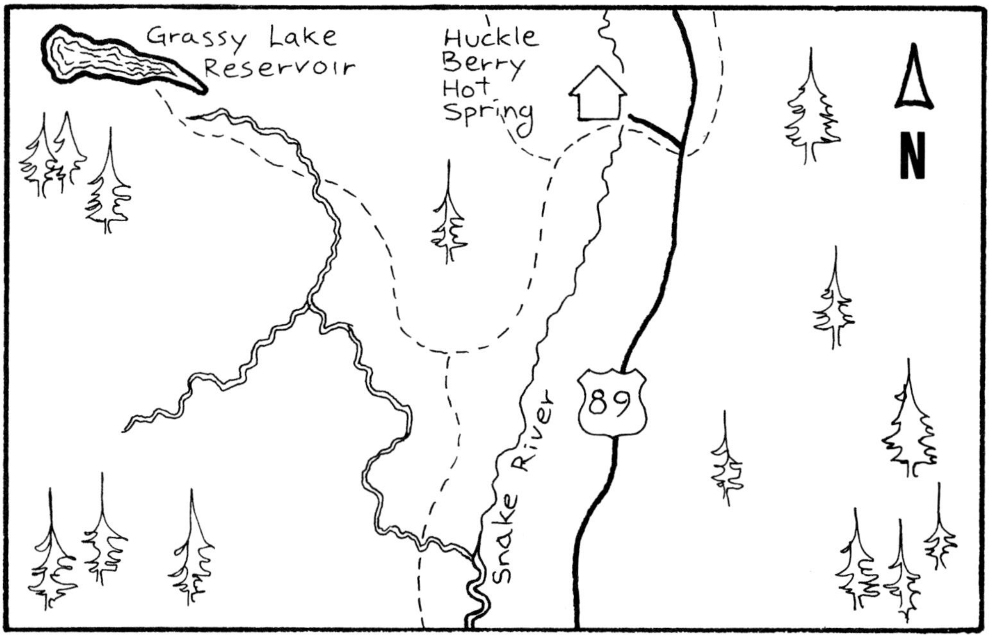

The enviable location of Flagg Ranch provides guests with access to two national parks. Ski touring at the base of the Teton Range, in Jackson Hole, is a memorable experience and the best Wyoming has to offer.

Triangle X Ranch

Location

On U.S. 89, 187 and 287, in Grand Teton National Park. 25 miles north of Jackson, Wyoming; 35 miles south of Yellowstone Park.

Accommodations

Winter capacity of 24 in 2, 3 and 4 bedroom cabins. Large cabin has 2 baths and living room. 2 rooms in lodge with bath down hall. $49 per person, per day, includes all meals, some guide service.

Trails and Snow Conditions

Marked and unmarked trails entire 55-mile length of Jackson Hole — Jenny, Taggart, Bradley Lakes; Oxbow Bend on Snake River; Ditch Creek, and more. Lots of flat touring area but also ridge and drainage climbs. Snowmobiles not permitted off designated roads. Snow and sun excellent. Elevation 6,700 feet.

Ski Rentals and Lessons

Lessons and guided tours at ranch. Rentals in Jackson at Skinny Skis.

Reservations

Make reservations during fall. No credit cards. Pets okay if they don't fight. They are not permitted to run loose.

Triangle X Ranch
Moose, WY 83012
(307) 733-2183

If the Grand Teton area isn't the snow capital of North America, or even of the United States, then surely it is the star of Wyoming.

It is difficult to imagine a more inspiring vision than those snow-covered granite spires impaling the jewel blue sky — the whole scene rising above an unlimited expanse of sparkling, powder snow. This park was made for ski touring.

In one of the most spectacular spots (of virtually endless spectacular spots) in the Tetons, is family-operated Triangle X Ranch. This homey spread is made up of superlatives — starting with the most gracious of hostesses, Louise Bertschy. The ranch has been in continuous family ownership since 1925. Louise has been there since 1935 and the Turners, who are her three sons and their families, reside and work on the ranch.

The ranch was once a working cattle outfit, but has been operated as a dude ranch for years. When the Park Service removed grazing rights 15 years ago, Triangle X switched from cattle to the raising of mules and horses. Nine years ago, the ranch opened for winter guests.

Above: Jenny Lake is a popular destination for Teton Park tourers. The summer boat dock makes a unique lunch stop. Below: The rambling complex of buildings at Triangle X Ranch includes log guest cabins.

"Get-you-started" guide service is provided at Triangle X. After that, you'll want to explore some trails on your own. From the end of the plowed road northwest of Moose, ski along the west side of Cottonwood Creek 4½ miles to Jenny Lake. From the same trail head, ski shorter (but steeper) distances to Taggart or Bradley Lakes.

Across the main highway from Moose Junction, turn east on Antelope Road. Park at the plowed-out area *before* you get to the Teton Science School. Walk past the school and ski up Ditch Creek, 6 miles one way.

Other tours range from gentle trails along the Snake River at Oxbow Bend

Above: Guest accommodations at Triangle X Ranch are meticulously cared for and well-winterized. Below: Ranch hostess Louise Bertschy opens her home to winter guests for meals and fireside gatherings.

north of Moran Junction, to a thundering run down the mountain from Teton Pass. The latter selection involves both telemarking and touring on an old road. You'll need a car shuttle from Heidelburg Inn (near Wilson) to the pass. In the willow areas along the river, you'll see wildlife, especially lots of moose. Do worship them from *afar.*

The Park Visitors' Center at Moose is open 8 to 5 year around. Maps and detailed trail information are available there. A museum in the Center graphically displays the salty history of Jackson Hole.

Although a program of naturalist ski tours conducted by the Park Service has been discontinued, snowshoe tours are still on.

Back at the ranch, there are machine-packed areas to ski, specifically on the flat "race track" site above the buildings.

Snowmobiles use Teton turf, too, but are restricted to roads. It's big country and there is room for all.

When you finish your day of touring, you'll still be able to gaze westward across the valley at the awesome sight of the Tetons — right from your cabin porch. The accommodations are some of the most lovingly maintained guest houses you'll ever find. Knotty pine interiors, yes. Unkempt, no. The wood shines and the furniture has not a scratch on it. Winterization care ensures that you will be warm on even the coldest day.

And from the back side of the cabin, toward the barn area, you'll see Park moose napping and contentedly munching pilfered hay in the ranch horse corrals.

In winter, meals are served centrally in the dining room of Louise's home. She can seat all guests at one time in the comfortable antique-filled room. Here you'll be able to review family photos and share in her life and experiences. In winter, the inviting fireplace in her dining area serves as a gathering place for ranch guests.

Most people stay at Triangle X three to eight days. Make reservations early — this is a popular spot. Summer reservations come in 1½ years in advance. And the business is virtually all by word of mouth.

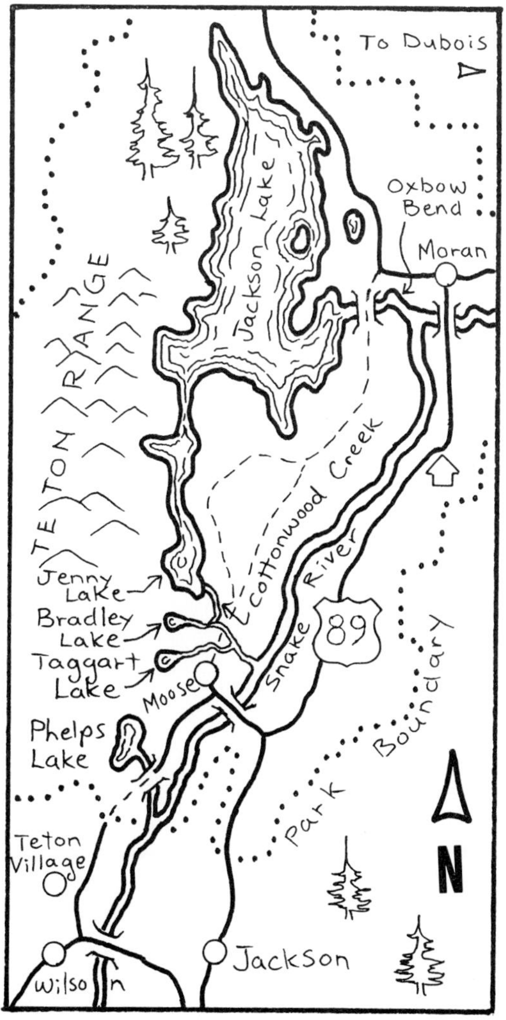

Western Motel

Location
In Jackson, Wyoming, at 225 South Glenwood, 2 blocks south of Broadway.

Accommodations
30 modern AAA motel units with color cable TV and phones. Winter group special, $36 per night for 2 includes wine welcome at owners' home, transportation to trail heads, guided ski tours and hot tub party.

Services
All services within walking distance.

Trails and Snow Conditions
Trail terrain for every ability level in Grand Teton National Park and nearby areas.

Ski Rentals and Lessons
Instruction and a variety of guide services available in immediate area. Rental arrangements may be made in advance with the motel.

Reservations
Major credit cards.
Western Motel
P.O. Box 1684
Jackson, WY 83001
(307) 733-3291

Harley Rolfe is concerned with more than changing bedsheets and making entries in reservation books. Proprietor of Jackson's Western Motel, he is not content with offering winter visitors color TV and an ice bucket. He likes to "deliver the country to guests."

Harley says that many visitors come to Jackson Hole to downhill ski and never see the inside of Grand Teton Park. It's his self-directed mission to rectify that oversight.

The wonders of the Park are Harley's favorite topic. He talks about the emotional experience of getting onto a snow-covered ridge to sit and look at the view. "For me, cross country skiing is secondary to the scenics. Skis are a means to get where I want to go." Downhiller Harley insists he is not a good Nordic skier, but knows where to go. He likes to custom tailor a trip depending on the interests and wishes of his guests. He'll arrange a 6:30 a.m. "sunrise on the Grand" photo trip to catch the few minutes of indigo and "the light when it's pink on the snow." That's real dedication.

Although he works extensively with tour agencies (the typical guest is a downhiller from the mid-west — most likely Chicago), Harley will provide the same TLC and show-and-tell for groups of ten or more. He will lead you on any number of tours or drop you off at a trail head.

Jackson, Wyoming's, Western Motel is a tip-of-the-iceberg gateway to the glories and wonders of the Tetons. Proprietor Harley Rolfe takes special pride in diverting downhillers onto skinny skis for a peek at the Park.

A picturesque snow-laden foot bridge adds to nature's charm at the foot of the spectacular Teton Mountains.

Engaged in a competitive commercial venture in an area which depends upon tourism for its life blood, Harley and his wife Paulie succeed without the use of customary promotion standards. They don't distribute advertising brochures, preferring instead to rely upon the traditional grapevine.

Though it's a cut-from-the-mold AAA motel, a clue to the Western's uniqueness lies in its brief description in a chamber of commerce pamphlet. Amidst listings of establishments variously detailed as "finest," "excellent," "convenient," "world's most . . . ," and "spectacular," the Western states simply, "Free cross-country arrangements and counseling. Cross-country areas well known to owner."

Harley can also provide information on other services in the area — and there are a bunch. Instruction and/or guides may be found at Powderhound Nordic, (307) 733-2181; Teton Village, (307) 733-3560; Jackson Hole Ski Tours, (307) 733-3056; Skinny Skis, (307) 733-6094, and Teton Mountain Touring, (208) 354-2768. Helicopter services are available at High Mountain Helicopter Skiing, (307) 733-3274.

Other local entertainments include horse sled rides near Jackson and dog sled expeditions at Kelly, (307) 733-9110.

In addition to Harley's tours, you can find easy gliding on your own at the Teton Village XC Center. They machine-set four kilometers of tracks — day fee, $3. And past Snow King, just east of town, is Cache Creek Trail, a gradual canyon floor tour. Also see trail information in listings for Flagg Ranch and Triangle X Ranch.

By day's end, you'll be ready to sample what Jackson, the town, offers. The Million Dollar Cowboy Bar is a must. You can't go to Jackson without at least poking your head through the door. It seems to be a bigger tourist attraction than the Park.

There is usually live music seven nights a week at several spots in town. The Silver Dollar Bar at the Wort Hotel is one of the more pleasant and least touristy meeting places.

For food, don't miss Jedediah's Sourdough, with an historic menu and cuisine that will definitely tempt you to extend your Jackson stay. They are open for all meals. A choice dinner spot is the Lame Duck with its "mixed-bag" oriental menu and excellent service. Prices are moderate at both restaurants.

A finishing touch (open until 10 p.m.) is the Teton Hot Pots at the north end of town. For $3.50 (or half price before 4 p.m.) you get use of the *hot* pool, *cold* plunge, sauna and showers.

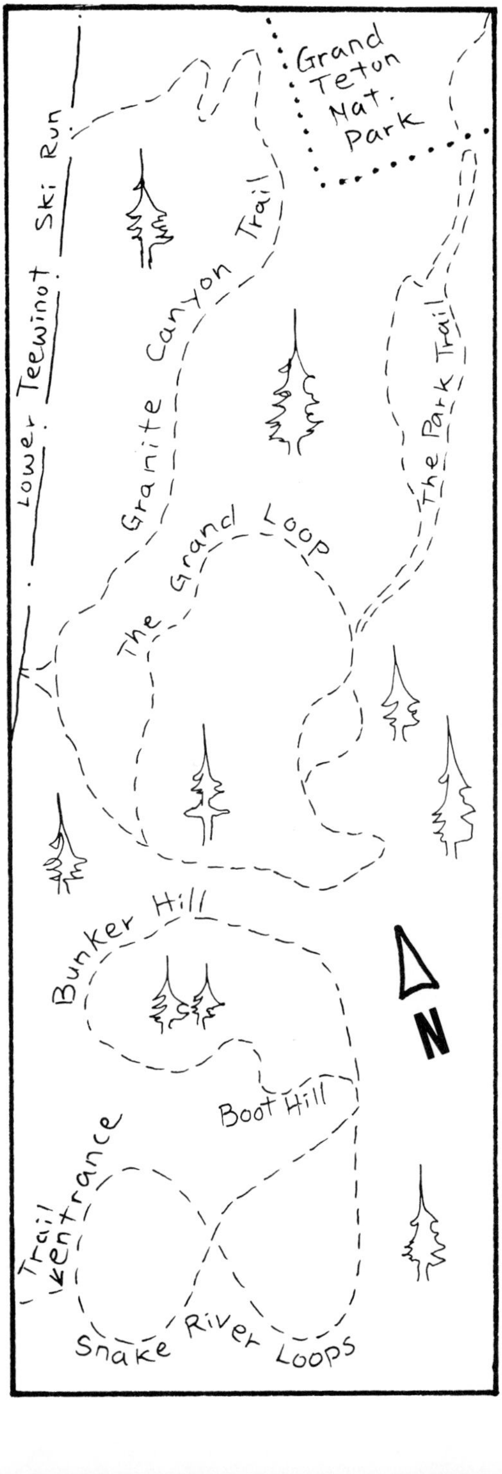

Camp Creek Inn

Location
On U.S. 187, 17 miles south of Jackson, Wyoming; 3 miles east of Hoback Junction.

Accommodations
9 cabins and A-frames, most with 2 double beds, sleep 2 to 5 people each. Electric heat, no kitchens. Capacity 30. Winter rates, $25 for a double; $3 each additional person.

Services
Restaurant and bar on premises. Gas and groceries at Hoback Junction.

Trails and Snow Conditions
Marked, non-maintained trails in Bridger-Teton National Forest. Intermediate to advanced ski levels. Share turf with snowmobiles. Base elevation, 6,000 feet.

Ski Rentals and Lessons
Guide service available. Nearest rentals and lessons at Jackson.

Reservations
Allow a week or two. MC, Visa. Pets okay.
Camp Creek Inn
Star Route 43B
Jackson, WY 83001
(307) 733-3099

Friendly, roadside stopover Camp Creek Inn, popular with the locals, is also a good Nordic base.

Your touring options in the area are twofold. 1) Set up a combination lodge stay and several-day ski trek package, or 2) take off on your own in Bridger-Teton National Forest.

At least two trails offer stimulating tours. Eight miles east of Camp Creek, turn north on the road to Granite Hot Springs. The 6-mile (one way) trail has a 1,500-foot elevation gain and leads to a natural hot spring. The 102 to 108 degree pool is operated by a concessionaire and a user fee is charged.

Another four miles down the highway, Cliff Creek Trail heads south. The trail returns to Highway 187, 23 miles down the road, so a car shuttle is in order. The terrain represents a lot of tough climbing and the full length of the trail is a two or three day venture. You are advised to ski with a guide if you don't know the area. Inn owner Roger Reece can help you with this.

The 1930 vintage log cafe/bar at Camp Creek is cozy, and food is good with homemade soup a winner. Accommodations are in roadside-motel type units or picturesque A-frames. Attractions include special buffets, occasional live music and holiday parties.

Above: The woodsy and warm cafe and bar at Camp Creek Inn is an inviting sight to winter travelers. Below: Highway lodging southeast of Jackson provides access to challenging mountain country.

White Pine Lodge

Location
Off Skyline Drive, 10 miles northeast of Pinedale, Wyoming; 65 miles southeast of Jackson, 100 miles north of Rock Springs.

Accommodations
10 motel units which sleep 4 to 5 people each, plus a 12-bed dorm provide accommodations for 65. No kitchens. In winter, open Friday and Saturday nights only. $34.50 for 4 or more in a room. Dorms $7/bed with bedding; $5/bed with your sleeping bag.

Services
Restaurant, bar — open Friday evening to Sunday afternoon — on premises. Groceries and gas in Pinedale.

Trails and Snow Conditions
60 km of machine-packed, marked trails on Bridger-Teton National Forest land. Trail heads at lodge. All ability levels.

Ski Rentals and Lessons
Rentals on premises. Lesson status uncertain — inquire.

Reservations
Several weeks in advance for Chirstmas vacation. Season, Thanksgiving to Easter. No credit cards. Pets okay.
White Pine Lodge
P.O. Box 833
Pinedale, WY 82941
(307) 367-2434 or 367-4121

"Trails passing through meadows, timber, open parks, and ridges provide views of both the lowlands of the Green River Valley and peaks of the Wind River Range." That's what the forest service map says of Skyline Drive Nordic Touring Trails at White Pine, but it doesn't begin to describe what you'll find.

The excellent trail system was established by the forest service five years ago. Tourers can snap on their skis right outside their door (there is so much snow, you'll almost need a shovel to get out) or buy a one-ride ticket for $1.50 to take a lift up that first hill.

A sampling of elevation levels in the area is 7,940 feet at Grouse Mountain trail head, 8,480 at the lodge, 9,330 at the top of the lift, and 10,340 at Photographers' Point. Trails are well marked with signboards at almost every intersection. Resort operators Terry and Barbara Pollard machine-pack the trails. But if they don't get around to it, one of the skiers will!

You may see a few snowmobiles here, but they definitely are in the minority. Machines are not permitted in the local valley or in adjacent Bridger Wilderness. And the typical canyonlands terrain is a bit rugged for them. The State of Wyoming grooms snowmobile trails in the Cora area, northwest of Pinedale, and that's hog heaven.

White Pine was established as a downhill area prior to World War II and has remained small and friendly. There is not the noise and hype common to downhill day lodges. Here you'll find a relaxed, quiet ambience. Ski tourers and downhillers wax their boards side by side in the 1967 vintage lodge.

Barbara and Terry have been at White Pine for six years. Terry is no stranger here. His grandfather built nearby Ponderosa Lodge and Terry once worked for a former owner of White Pine. The resort is a popular guest ranch and hunting lodge in other seasons.

Downhillers and Nordic tourers alike share the low-key day lodge at White Pine, in the high country north of Pinedale, Wyoming. Both dorms and motel style rooms are available on winter weekends at the friendly ski area.

The Pollards are having fun right along with their visitors. Their restaurant, the "Wandering Wapiti" (Wyoming elk) converts from a snack bar by day to a tablecloth and candlelight dining room in the evening. The menu offers such delights as "Sweetgrass Women," the chef salad, and "Whipper Snapper" portions. The history behind the "Captain Bonneville" is that "the good captain pushed (and shoved) his trusty men on a 100-mile forced march to get these barbecued ribs, dripping with western-style sauce, refusing to wash his hands for a week afterwards while he licked off every delectable trace." And the feast is available in three sizes: trappers, Indians and pony dancers.

The Wind River Mountains resort is the site of annual Nordic competition for high school and intermountain juniors. The race course is considered so tough that some coaches won't use it. But training has paid off for local athletes. Pinedale is home for a number of Olympic hopefuls and at least one U.S. team member, Latner Straley.

Pinedale is also the home of cutter races, a sport almost exclusive to Wyoming and Idaho. Years ago people began racing two-horse sled, or "cutter," teams. In recent years, dry-track, two-wheeled chariots have all but replaced the cutter blades. Colorfully-decked thoroughbreds and quarter horses are used for the quick-getaway, quarter-mile dashes. They run flat out, and are flying 40 to 50 miles per hour by the time they cross the finish line.

The two-day Wyoming championship event in Pinedale sees 20 or 30 races per day and is scheduled for the first weekend of March.

If you can't drive, do a little flying yourself. Pinedale's 7,200 foot airstrip is open year around.

Pinedale is home of the annual Wyoming championship cutter races, held each March. At nearby White Pine Lodge, tourers will find an excellent system of set xc tracks in a quiet forested area adjacent to the Bridger Wilderness.

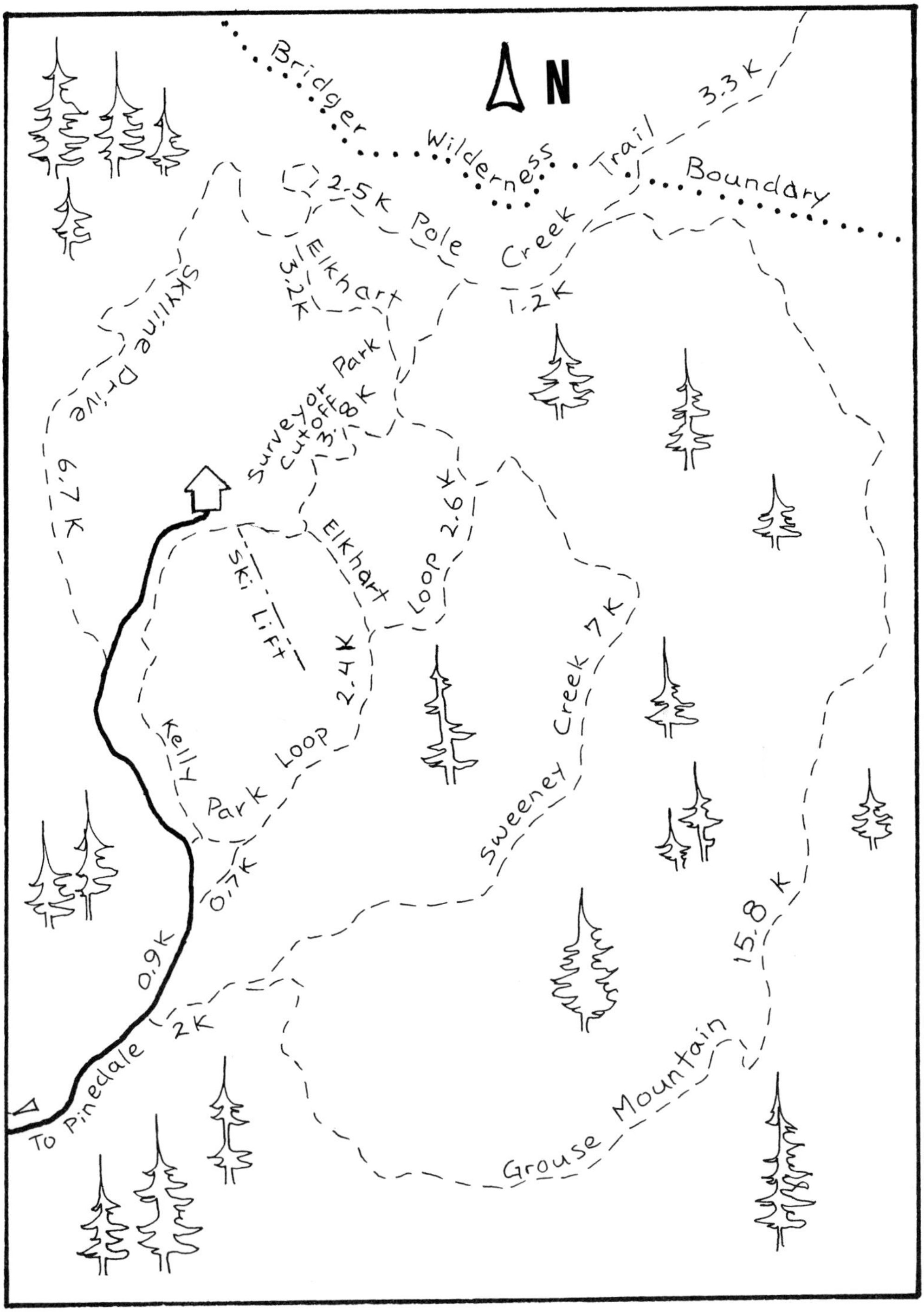
N
Bridger Wilderness Boundary
Trail 3.3 K
2.5 K Pole Creek
1.2 K
Elkhart 3.2 K
Skyline Drive 6.7 K
Surveyor Park 3.1 K
Cutoff .8 K
Elkhart Loop 2.6 K
Ski Lift
Kelly Park Loop 2.4 K
0.7 K
Sweeney Creek 7 K
15.8 K
0.9 K
2 K
To Pinedale
Grouse Mountain

Rawhide Ranch

Location
2 miles off Sunlight Basin Road (County Road 296); 25 miles west of Wyoming 120; 42 miles northwest of Cody.

Accommodations
Dorm-style units with bunks, central baths and wood heat. Bring warm sleeping bags. One cabin has kitchen facility with wood cook stove. $25 per night includes breakfast, supper and to-go lunches. $10.50 without meals.

Services
Family-style meals. All other services at Cody.

Trails and Snow Conditions
Ski out your door on non-maintained trails.

Ski Rentals and Lessons
No rentals. Lesson status uncertain.

Reservations
Let them know in advance. No credit cards. Pets okay.
Rawhide Ranch
Box 1810
Cody, WY 82414
(307) 587-2061

Getting there is half the fun! Turn off Highway 120 onto Sunlight Basin Road, about 17 miles north of Cody, and you're on the track into a different world. The highway map won't give you a clue, but the Shoshone National Forest map conspicuously outlines a rather extensive set of switchbacks dropping down into Sunlight Basin.

The first half of the route is a scenic wonder in itself — top of the world outlook, red cliffs, craggy canyons. But after you pass Dead Indian Summit, at 8,673 feet, you're in for a really spectacular sight. Shimmering mountains to the west are "replicas" of Alaskan ice field ranges. Opening 2,000 feet below, if you dare take your eyes from the road, you'll see flat Sunlight Basin, enclosed by rugged, rocky walls. Rawhide Ranch is nestled in trees just above the sunny valley floor.

The road to the ranch seems long at first, but is well maintained and not dangerous. There is an unlimited grab bag of beautiful surprises at every bend.

Rawhide Ranch was a summer-only operation until 1981-82, and has been owned and operated as a kids' ranch for the last five years by Cynthia and Jay Devereaux. Summer cooks Beth Ahren and Rhonda Harmon, both xc skiers, wanted to try their hand at offering a program for fellow winter people and have set up a package of hearty home-cooked meals and rustic lodging at the sprawling ranch. Both European and American plans are available.

They also are identifying and providing information on area trails. The ranch setting is at 6,800 feet.

Rawhide is one of only two Wyoming lodges which cater specifically to xc skiers in winter. The skier utilization program is new and chances are changes will be made as time goes by. The ranch is a natural for groups, but is also a good choice for the tourer who *really* wants quiet isolation — as well as sunshine, quaint charm and a wondrous unusual kind of beauty.

The road to Rawhide Ranch, long and snaky, descends 2,000 feet on its final approach to Sunlight Basin. The route, north of Cody, Wyoming, is rife with breathtaking pristine mountain panoramas.

Pahaska Tepee

Location
On U.S. 14, 16, 20. 2 miles east of Yellowstone Park entrance, 50 miles west of Cody, Wyoming. *Winter access from east only.*

Accommodations
51 cabins sleep 2-6 people each. Fireplaces in some cabins. Hostel rooms accommodate 1-5 people in bunks. Bring sleeping bags for hostel. Resort capacity 160. Hostel, $10 per night. Cabins, $32-38. One complete house, with kitchen, rents for $85 per night.

Services
Restaurant, bar, gift shop, gas, groceries on premises.

Trails and Snow Conditions
Virtually unlimited break-your-own trail mileage in Shoshone National Forest, Yellowstone Park and North Absaroka Wilderness area. Some trails machine-packed.

Ski Rentals and Lessons
Rentals on premises. Instruction available by advance arrangement.

Reservations
Major credit cards. Pets okay, but subject to forest service regulations.
Pahaska Tepee
Box 2370
Cody, WY 82414
(307) 587-5536

"Man with long hair." That's English for the Sioux word, Pahaska.

Pahaska Tepee, a two-story log structure, was built as a 1901 hunting lodge by the long-haired Buffalo Bill Cody — on property given to him by the Sioux.

Nowadays, the entire complex of the newer main lodge, cabins, Cody's original lodge, and outbuildings is referred to as Pahaska Tepee.

Cody built his lodge to host friends and as an office, and later operated it as a hotel. One of his notable visitors was Teddy Roosevelt. Roosevelt named his "rough riders" after terminology used by Cody in his wild west extravaganza billings.

Some of Cody's furnishings remain in the building, which in recent years has been used as a summer tourist stop.

To get the full flavor of Buffalo Bill country, you'll want to make a pilgrimage to the town of Cody — 50 miles east of Pahaska Tepee.

Buffalo Bill Cody built the original Pahaska Tepee, a log hunting lodge, in 1901. His furnishings are still housed in the rustic structure. One of Cody's more notable guests was Teddy Roosevelt.

Buffalo Bill was instrumental in establishing Cody in 1897 and his mark is evident everywhere in the area. A must-stop in Cody is the beautifully maintained Irma Hotel. Buffalo Bill constructed the stone edifice in 1902 and named it after his daughter. Queen Victoria, charmed by his free-wheeling Wild West Show and personal magnetism, presented Bill with the magnificent carved cherry wood back bar, which still dominates the large dining area. The gorgeous piece, made in France, was shipped to New York by steamer, to Red Lodge, Montana, by rail, then by horse-drawn freight wagon to Cody.

The important Buffalo Bill Historical Center is not open December through February, but if your visit is in late February, you'll be in time for the annual Buffalo Bill Birthday Ball.

To give you a clue as to the goings-on in this part of Wyoming, the Cody Yellow Pages include listings for "Oil Well Services", "Rodeos" . . . and "Ranches" — 82 of them!

Friendly and interesting as Cody (the town) is, you'll need to head westward to find snow.

At 6,668-foot elevation Pahaska Tepee, you can ski out your cabin door. Take off behind the complex and head up the North Fork of the Shoshone River, or ski east along the highway, across the bridge, and turn north at the sign which marks Sunlight Trail. This leads almost immediately into the North Absaroka Wilderness. The footing can be tricky, depending on snow conditions. The trail itself terminates at Cooke City, Montana, 100 miles north, so you won't lack for distance!

The highway into the Park ends under uncleared snow at Pahaska Tepee so you can ski on this road too. You may

A new lodge was built as a visitor's stop two miles east of Yellowstone Park in the late 50's. The prominent building accommodates a restaurant and gift shop. Overnight guests stay in cabins and a dorm.

have to share it with snowmobiles on weekends, but at least it will be "groomed." About 2,000 snow machines go through Yellowstone daily, but Pahaska is probably the least used winter entrance. The area is fairly congestion-free and well-controlled.

The late 50's era main lodge back at Pahaska Tepee is a lovely big structure housing an extensive gift shop, the "Mountain Fountain" snack counter, a cozy bar, and a dining room graced by a rock fireplace with *massive* raised hearth.

Furnishings include straight-backed dining chairs and bar stools adorned with small carved bighorn sheep heads and burl wood lounge chairs.

Guest accommodations run the gamut from multi-bunk rooms to a completely furnished modern house.

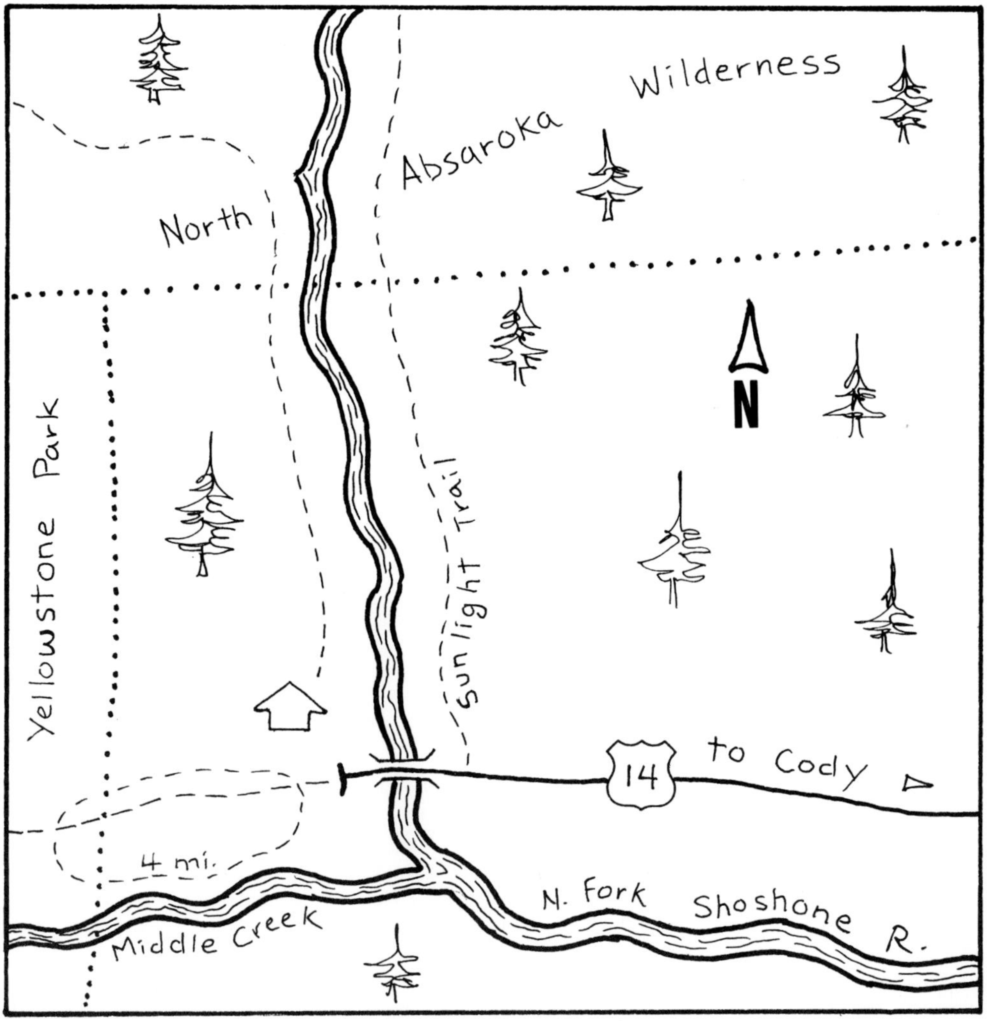

Old Faithful Snow Lodge

Location
Depart by snow coach (30 mile trip) from West Yellowstone, Montana on U.S. 20 and 191; 80 miles south of Bozeman; 100 miles north of Idaho Falls, Idaho. Snow coach fare, $36 round trip. (Fare to Old Faithful from Park south entrance, $47.84)

Accommodations
Lodging in cabins with private baths or in lodge rooms with or without bath. No cooking. Rates start at $23.50 plus tax per night for two.

Services
Restaurant, bar at lodge. All other services at West Yellowstone.

Trails and Snow Conditions
Ski on marked summer trails or break your own trail virtually anywhere through the Park. Usually excellent snow conditions. Elevation, 7,362 feet.

Ski Rentals and Lessons
Rentals, lessons and guide service available at Snow Lodge or in West Yellowstone at Rendezvous Ski Shop and Yellowstone Nordic Wilderness Shop.

Reservations
6 months in advance usually necessary; 1 year for holidays.
AmEx, DC, MC, Visa. No pets.
Old Faithful Snow Lodge
Yellowstone Park Division
TWA Services, Inc.
Yellowstone National Park, WY 82190-0165
(307) 344-7311

Yellowstone in winter is a spectacular sight! The plumy spray from Old Faithful blends with glittering white snow — against a cerulean backdrop of Wyoming sky. Ski to gorgeous Morning Glory Pool, aptly named for shape and color, and again view the beauty of winter blue and white.

The most overwhelming aspect of the experience is the number of elk and bison visible everywhere. The animals are not nearly so evident in summer. But in winter, when snow forces them to range at lower elevation, there they are — along your entire snow coach route as well as in the geyser basins area. Ski amid the geysers and hot pools and you'll have to detour around the game — they like the geothermal fringe benefits, too.

Remember — no matter how close you are able to get (you'll be able to almost touch them) they are *wild* animals. Unpredictable, self-protective, and *very* strong.

You'll also see trumpeter swans. These birds, which sometimes grow to 35 pounds, were all but extinct in the mid-30's when only 26 specimens remained. Their numbers are now increasing — look for them on the rivers.

Top: A common sight to Yellowstone winter visitors is the huge bison. The animals use their massive heads to burrow through deep snow for forage. Below: Skiers and bison share the warm geyser basins area.

You'll see Canada Geese (they like to follow around the bison and elk), water ouzels and possibly bald eagles and moose, depending on your route. If the snow has started to recede, you may see deer.

There is one rather sizable ante for all this splendor. Snowmobiles are permitted on the highways of Yellowstone and your imagination simply can't conjure up the level of Park utilization by these machines. You'll not have to contend with them on the trails, but you must get some distance away from the Old Faithful area before the constant buzzing subsides.

The snowmobile rental business around the Park is absolutely thriving and the road in front of the Snow Lodge looks like a Cecil B. DeMille extravaganza, complete with cast of thousands.

Magnificent and historic Old Faithful Inn is not open during winter. The modern Snow Lodge, operated by TWA Services (Park concessionaires for food, lodging and transportation) provides comfortable housing in the same area.

Nordic activities are well organized at the Snow Lodge and trail information and maps are profusely available.

Top: There is no machine shortage in West Yellowstone or at Old Faithful, or anywhere along the route in between. Below: The Old Faithful Snow Lodge is a mighty popular destination for winter travelers.

In addition to the ski tours in the Park, for example the 6-mile round-trip Morning Glory Pool route, or 17-mile round trip to Fairy Falls, a few ski trails have been designated near the town of West Yellowstone. So while you're waiting for your snow coach departure, you can do some touring in that area. You probably won't want to spend much time there, however, because the town is literally occupied by snowmobilers. In fact, it is billed as the "Snowmobile Capital of the World."

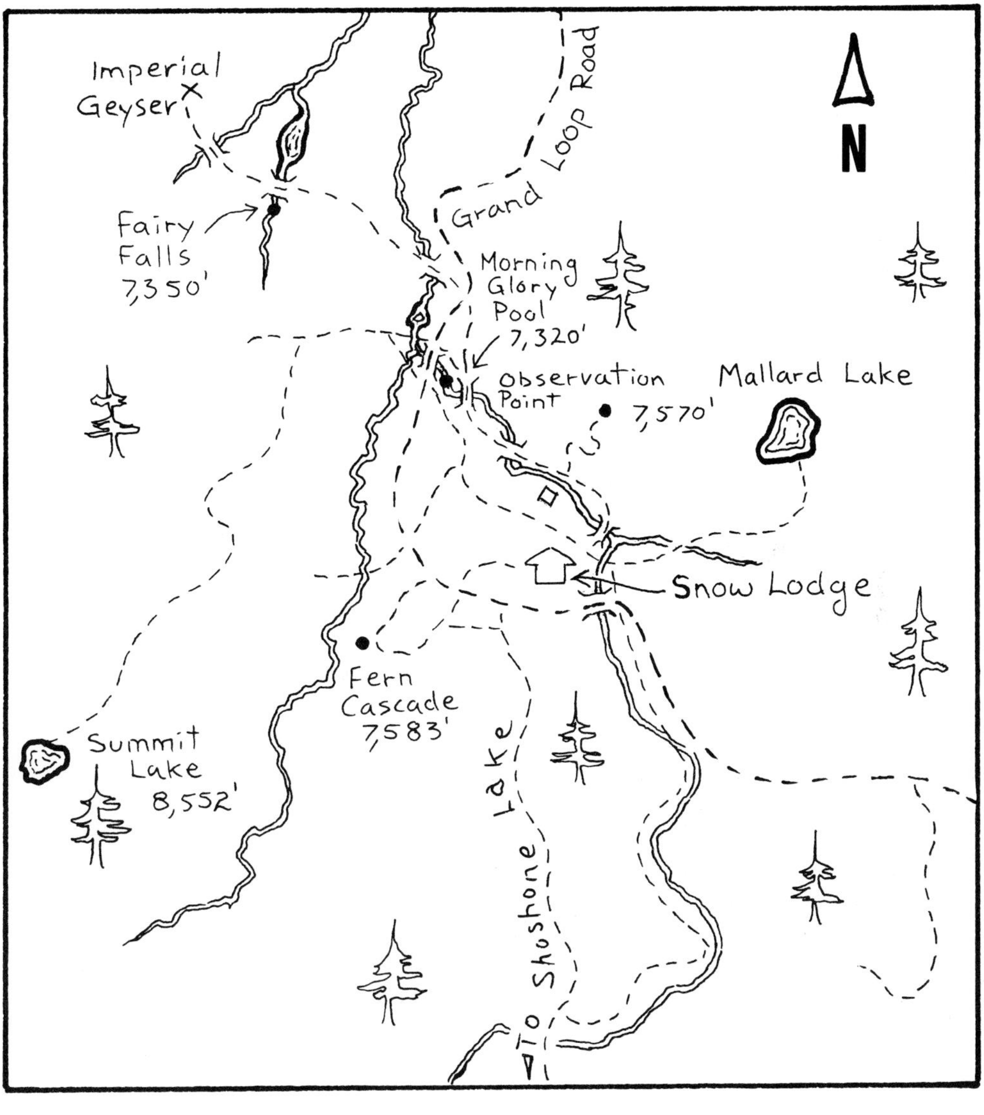

128 Wind River Ranch Ski Lodge

Location

On U.S. 26 and 287, 17 miles west of Dubois, Wyoming; 60 miles southeast of Yellowstone Park, 92 miles west of Lander.

Accommodations

10 lodge rooms with bath down hall, sleep 2 to 4 people each. Cabin facilities are modern, rustic or "super rustic". The latter has no water, no toilet and is heated by fireplace. All cabins have fireplaces and kitchens, although one unit has no sink. Bedding, dishes furnished. Capacity 44. $35 per person for 1 night, or $25 per for a 3-night package, includes lodging, meals, lessons and guide service.

Services

Meals, sauna on premises. Restaurant, bar, game room, gas at nearby motel. Groceries at Dubois.

Trails and Snow Conditions

Ski out your door onto 15 miles of marked and set-track trails. Ski one way 10 miles from Togwotee Pass down to lodge on unmarked trail (guides available). Lots of wide open meadows. Snow that won't quit.

Ski Rentals and Lessons

Ski rentals in Dubois — or let lodge know in advance and they'll get them for you. Complete instruction and guide service at lodge.

Reservations

2 weeks; longer for holidays. Airport pick-up available. Major credit cards. Pets okay.
Wind River Ranch Ski Lodge
P.O. Box 278
Dubois, WY 82513
(307) 455-2721

Here is the best of all worlds in Wyoming. You're a xc skier? This is your own exclusive place. Se habla ski touring.

According to ski lodge manager Lenora Cusumano, "It snows a little bit every night." (And it's sunny a lot every day.) Even when virtually all other areas were bereft of snow in 1980-81, Wind River Ranch was wallowing in it. This winter haven at 8,000 feet is just down the eastern slope of Continental Divide summit, 9,658-foot Togwotee Pass. The 165-acre privately-owned Wind River Mountains property is surrounded by the Shoshone National Forest.

When you arrive at road-front "Wind River Ranch," note that of several signs, the one pertaining to the ski lodge directs you "across the river." Drive on by the motel in the foreground.

Salt Lake surgeon Mac Davenport owns both the motel and the ranch, but opera-

An array of lodging choices awaits the visitor to Wind River Ranch Ski Lodge. The northwestern Wyoming guest ranch provides complete touring services near 9,658-foot Togwotee Pass in the Wind River Range.

tions (no pun intended) are separate. The motel is the first building you come to. It's a low log structure with a really fine restaurant, comfortable bar and more than ample game room. The restaurant and bar are usually closed Monday through Wednesday during winter.

The skier's digs, however, are across the river and through the moose willows. You'll be amazed at the freshness of the interior. It has "ranch" decor — with handmade pine and hickory furniture, massive stone fireplace — but the hardwood floors look like they have never been walked on.

Meals are served family style at a long polished wood table at one end of the kitchen. Trail lunches are packed to go. Don't be surprised if, upon your arrival, a few bottles of wine are uncorked.

Your ski vacation will be truly customized at Wind River Ranch. "We'll do whatever people want," says Lenora, of the instruction/guide service. Lenora and two other staff members can provide services ranging from getting you onto skis to telemark coaching and map and compass training. There also are moonlight tours.

Before she came to Wyoming from Oswego, New York, Lenora owned a successful restaurant specializing in a little bit of everything she "liked but couldn't get in upstate New York" — Mexican, oriental, Greek dishes. You'll

The main ski lodge at Wind River Ranch is a haven set aside especially for Nordic tourers. The mint-condition, three-story structure was built by local tie hacks, the now-obsolete artisans of hand hewn railroad ties.

be glad to know Lenora has a hand in the cooking at Wind River's ski lodge.

Ambience here is friendly and casual. Owner Mac can't stay away. He commutes virtually every weekend, 18 hours round trip, just to "sit in the woods" or "cut a tree."

Some serious stuff gets done here, too. During the annual Dubois February winter carnival, Nordic events are held at Wind River Ranch. They include such formidable competition as the beer slalom.

One of two Wyoming lodges specifically seeking Nordic clientele, Wind River entered the ski touring business during 1980-81 and already it's a big, but definitely modest star. Don't miss this one.

Xc spoken here.

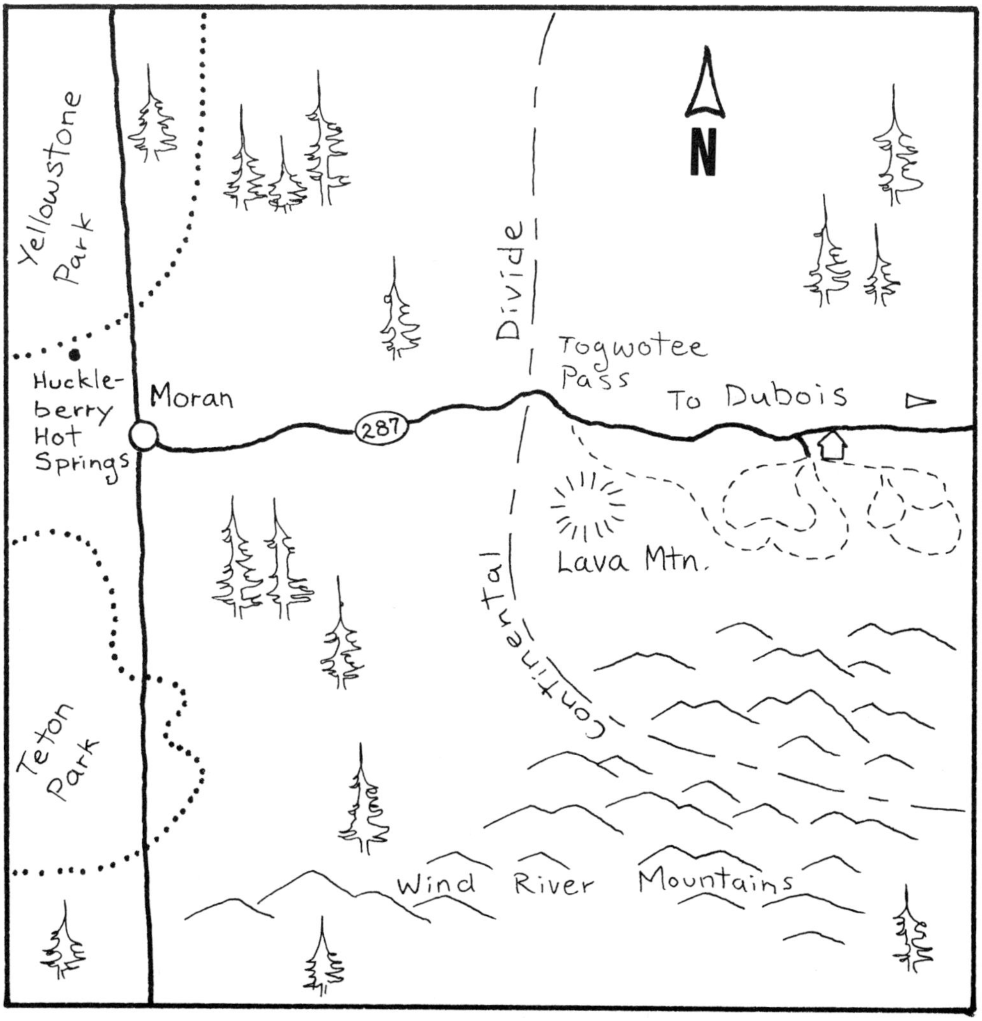

Bear Lodge

Location

At Burgess Junction, on U.S. 14/14-A, 48 miles east of Greybull, Wyoming. 50 miles west of Sheridan. *(Highway 14-A to Lowell closed in winter.)*

Accommodations

8 motel units each with 2 double beds. (1 room has 3 double beds). Capacity 34. Closed Wednesdays. $24.50 plus tax for 1 or 2; $2.50 per extra person.

Services

Restaurant, bar, gas, souvenirs, limited groceries.

Trails and Snow Conditions

Marked trails at Antelope Butte downhill area 14 miles south, and in the vicinity of Blue Spruce Cafe, 1½ miles south. Break your own trail anywhere else, but *do* avoid snowmobile tracks. Also see Arrowhead Lodge for additional trail information.

Ski Rentals and Lessons

Nearest rentals, Antelope Butte Ski Area. Also available in Sheridan. No lessons.

Reservations

Exxon, MC, Visa. Pets discouraged.
Bear Lodge
Rt. 2 Box 445
Sheridan, WY 82801
(307) 655-2444

The top of the Big Horns. That is literally where you'll stay at picturesque old Bear Lodge.

From here you can see for miles across the sparsely-treed rolling terrain of what otherwise is a rather flat-topped range of mountains. There are pinnacles farther south, in the Cloud Peak Wilderness Area, so the view is lovely. But in your more immediate area the contour is relatively flat. Bear Lodge is at 8,300 feet, less than 700 feet down from the nearby summit at Granite Pass.

Big Horn Mountains (capital B, capital H) were named for the bighorn sheep (one word, lower case) which once were populous in the high country of the mountain range.

Sunshine and blue skies are the real plus here, and the snow is great. You can ski out the door of your room, but do watch out for the machines. This country is closely-guarded by snowmobilers — they even pre-groom their own trails. Best to ski on the marked xc trails at Antelope Butte or at Blue Spruce Cafe. Blue Spruce is supportive of skiers and hosts an annual xc set-track race on the premises in mid-February.

Motel type rooms at the rustic log lodge are bright and clean.

Major services are most easily accessed at Sheridan, at the eastern base of the mountains. Despite the proximity to snow in the Big Horns, Sheridan really hasn't heard of xc skiing yet. Your strange attire, particularly your funny-toed shoes, may draw long stares. A more common wintertime sight on eastern Wyoming sidewalks is pointy-toed overshoes. Designed to fit over cowboy boots, the galoshes are readily available at any shoe shop or outdoor store.

If you feel a bit out of place, go to Perkins Restaurant at the south end of town for genuine friendliness and TLC.

Rambling Bear Lodge, at the junction of U.S. 14 and 14-A, offers a lofty log perch at the top of Wyoming's Big Horn Mountains. The 8,300-foot elevation inn, in the land of sun and snow, is near Antelope Butte Ski area.

Arrowhead Lodge

Location
On U.S. 14, 47 miles west of Sheridan, Wyoming; 27 miles southwest of Dayton; 50 miles east of Greybull. *(14-A from Lowell closed in winter.)*

Accommodations
8 motel units sleep 2-4 people each. Winter closure Monday and Tuesday. Rates start at $24 for 2.

Services
Restaurant, bar, souvenirs, gas, snacks. Nearest groceries 3 miles west at Bear Lodge or Blue Spruce Cafe.

Trails and Snow Conditions
Ski out your door. Break trail or ski unplowed roads. *Watch out for snowmobiles.* Marked xc trails at Antelope Butte, 17 miles west.

Ski Rentals and Lessons
Rentals at Antelope Butte or Big Horn Mountain Shop, Sheridan.

Reservations
MC, Visa.
Arrowhead Lodge
P.O. Box 267
Dayton, WY 82836
(307) 655-2388

At the Owl's Nest Restaurant, even the noodles are homemade in the homemade chicken soup.

And there is a real owl's nest on the wall.

It's a cozy place, with painted red furniture, miscellaneous antiques and much owl memorabilia.

The rest of Arrowhead Lodge is a cozy place, too. Rooms are comfortable, the main lodge always is scented of a wood fire and the bartender is jolly. Behind the bar is a sign bearing the capital letters "YCJCYAQFTJB." Underneath follows "TMTY." Don't ask. It means "Your curiosity just cost you a quarter for the juke box. The managment thanks you."

The hat collection — almost 300 — in the bar is worth studying.

Each owner of Arrowhead Lodge has contributed a bit to the resort. The establishment began as a boys' camp in 1910. A lodge was built in the mid-20's. Additions, including the dining room, kitchen and bar and motel units, were installed over a period of almost 20 years, from the mid-40's.

Current owners Del and Betty Englen and Jim and Laural Pittman, took over Arrowhead five years ago, superseding their partnership in a Cheyenne motel. Each of the four individuals contributes a different area of expertise to the operation.

Big Horn Mountains resort, Arrowhead Lodge, is in the thick of snow country and attracts both skiers and snowmobilers. Dedicated cross country ski trails may be found at Antelope Butte Ski Area; other trails must be shared.

At 7,600 feet up in the Big Horn Mountains, there is plenty of snow. Try skiing 3 miles east of the lodge at Sibley Lake. Or ski toward Black Mountain Lookout either from the lake or on the unplowed Black Mountain Road. Forest service maps are available at the lodge.

A good tour choice is to Blue Spruce Cafe, at the 8,300-foot level, and back again, a round trip of 4 to 5 miles. See the Bear Lodge listing for additional trail information.

A word of caution is in order. No matter where you go in the territory, except for the xc trail at Antelope Butte, you'll find snow machines. They were here first, and don't you forget it.

Terrain at 7,600-foot Arrowhead Lodge is sparsely wooded with both rolling hills and steep contours. Tour choices include a romp to a fire lookout and glides across frozen Sibley Lake and the top of the Big Horns.

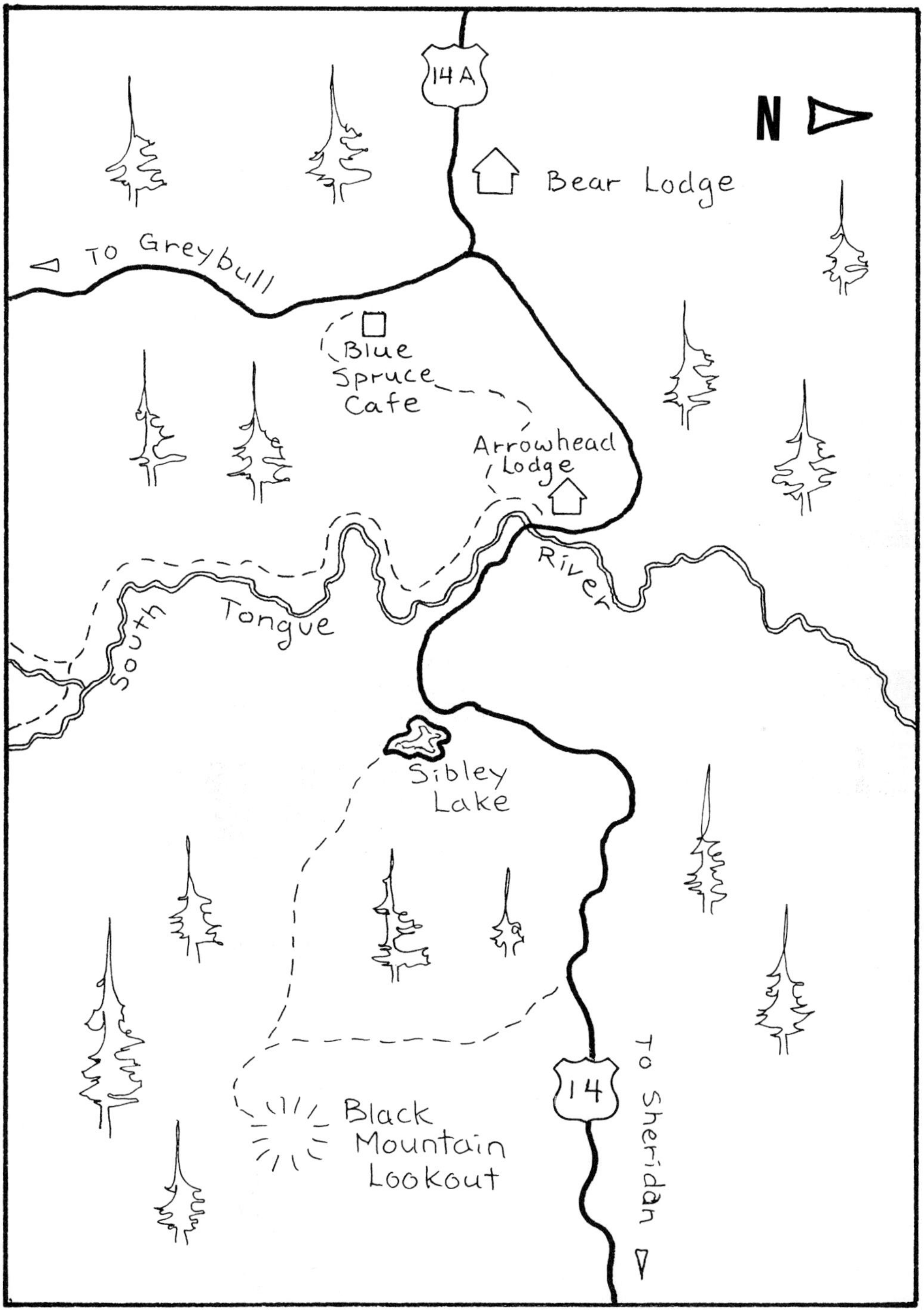
14A
N
Bear Lodge
To Greybull
Blue Spruce Cafe
Arrowhead Lodge
River
South Tongue
Sibley Lake
Black Mountain Lookout
14
To Sheridan

Meadowlark Resort

Location
On U.S. 16, 42 miles west of Buffalo, Wyoming. 21 miles east of Ten Sleep; 47 miles east of Worland.

Accommodations
14 cabins, 6 cottages and 6 motel units sleep 1-10 each. Carpeted motel rooms are modern with all conveniences except kitchens. Cabins are *rustic* with no indoor plumbing. Central shower house. Bedding and towels are furnished; dishes and cooking utensils are not. $3.50 extra for cooking in cabins and cottages. Rates start at $20 for 1 or 2 people.

Services
Restaurant, bar, gas at resort. Nearest groceries, Deer Haven Lodge, 3 miles west.

Trails and Snow Conditions
About 12 miles of marked and groomed trails at Willow Park, 2 miles west of resort. All ability levels. Meadows, trees, view of Cloud Peak Wilderness mountains.

Ski Rentals and Lessons
Rentals at Meadowlark downhill area, 1 mile east. No lessons.

Reservations
In advance preferably. MC, Visa. Pets okay.
Meadowlark Resort
P.O. Box 37
Ten Sleep, WY 82442
(307) 366-2424

To the Indians who frequently traveled the 20-day trail between Bridger, Montana, and what is now Casper, Wyoming, the midway overnight was "ten sleep". The name stuck.

A few miles east of Ten Sleep, now a town in the prodigious Big Horn Mountains, is Meadowlark Lake and shoreline Meadowlark Resort.

The area accommodates many and is a popular gathering place for winter enthusiasts. Some of the habitues are recreational snow machiners, so be prepared for a wild time.

The snowmobilers are a friendly lot in this section of the Big Horns. Ironically, skiers have a trail system all to themselves. The forest service has done a really fine job of cutting, marking, grooming and maintaining a network of loops heading from Willow Park Picnic Ground. The area is off limits to snowmobiles.

A short tour — following the signs to "cabin" — will bring you to a popular meadow lunch stop. Locals report that the old cabin, now in a state of collapse, was built by Jake Johnson, a Big Horn recluse. He built about 15 log structures in the area and according to a local spokesman, "would shoot you if you ran into him." Not to worry. Jake has been at the big log cabin in the sky for 30 years.

Terrain and trail variety is excellent and "you are here" maps are placed at every intersection.

Above: If skiing becomes a bore, the Willow Park trail head in Wyoming's Big Horn Mountains provides alternative recreational opportunities. Below: Lakeside Meadowlark Lodge rests at 8,700 feet elevation.

But — the system is in peril. USFS budgets are being whittled ever smaller and the future of Willow Park, the best xc area in the Big Horns, is a distressing unknown at this time.

Perhaps Oscar, the "mischievous entity" described by Meadowlark Resort owner Maxine Brauher, will play a few tricks and make money reappear for the forest service. Oscar is a ghost who reportedly frequented the resort for years and 'lifted' and then replaced a hefty sum of money from the wallet of a customer.

Maxine, who owns the resort with her husband Dale, has researched Oscar's shenanigans back to 1942. His antics have included the turning on and off of propane tanks, loud stomping, but worst — and the final straw for one employee — the windy playing of bag pipes.

Well before Oscar's time, an English woman, Ms. Isabel Teasdale, obtained the first forest service permit to operate the "Meadowlark Resort and Tea Room." Her lodge, which later burned, was at lake's edge. The exisiting log structure, near the highway, was built in 1934.

From the resort, you can view the downhill races (with binoculars) across the frozen lake. The resort is at an elevation of 8,700 feet, about 1,000 feet lower than the summit at nearby Powder River Pass.

If Oscar should jumble your reservations at Meadowlark, very similar accommodations are available 3 miles west at Deer Haven Lodge. You won't find respite from the "sledders" there, however. For Deer Haven reservations, write to P.O. Box 121, Ten Sleep, WY 82442. (307) 366-2449.

Lodging at Meadowlark Resort is available in motel units and picturesque lakeside cabins. Ski rentals are available across the lake at a downhill ski area. An excellent marked trail system offers a view of Cloud Peak Wilderness.

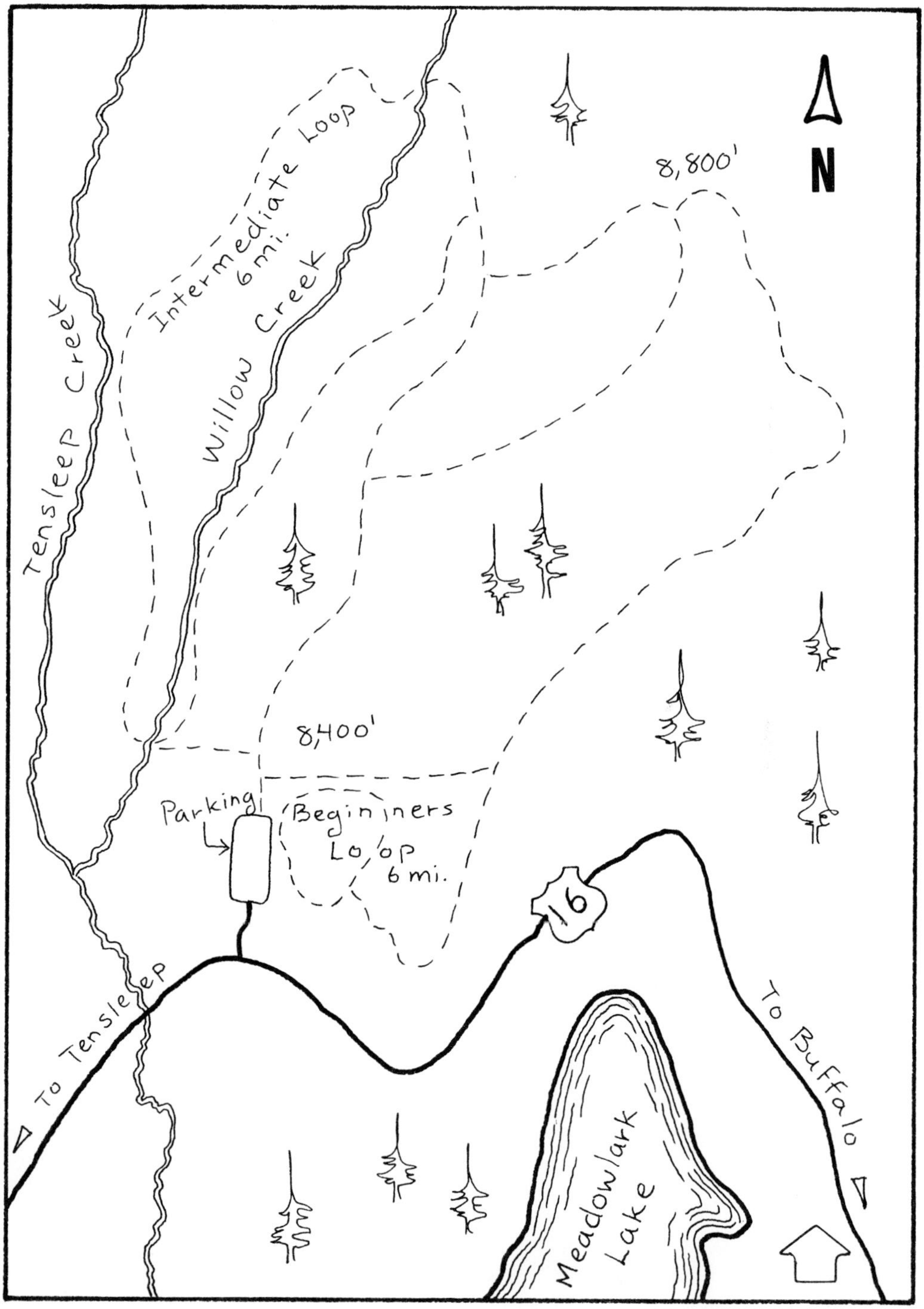
N
8,800'
Intermediate Loop
6 mi.
Willow Creek
Tensleep Creek
8,400'
Parking
Beginners
Loop
6 mi.
16
To Tensleep
To Buffalo
Meadowlark
Lake

Esterbrook Lodge

Location
At end of Esterbrook Road, 27 miles south of Douglas, Wyoming; 80 miles southeast of Casper.

Accommodations
Esterbrook can house 25 people in rustic cabins, each accommodating 2 to 6. Heat, but no running water; no kitchens. $25 per night for 1 or 2; $5 each additional.

Services
Restaurant, bar. Nearest services Esterbrook, or 21 miles to Glendo, if road is passable.

Trails and Snow Conditions
Miles of nearby trails marked by the forest service must be shared with snowmobilers. Snow (lack of) can be a problem some winters and the area tends to be windy. Elevation 6,600 feet.

Ski Rentals and Lessons
No lessons. Rentals at DJ's Sports in Douglas.

Reservations
No credit cards. Pets okay on leash.
Esterbrook Lodge
Rt. 6
Douglas, WY 82633
No phone

"The original home of the Jackalope" is a title claimed, according to State of Wyoming travel writers, by the Laramie Mountains community of Douglas. In Wyoming, the Jackalope is so omnipresent it would appear to be the state animal. In virtually every commercial establishment, there hangs the mounted head of the creature — jackrabbit head and ears, with small mule deer antlers. These tacky taxidermy mutations sell for about $65, and business must be good. An Evanston entrepreneur, one Alexander Ragtime, has even published a book on the subject. He calls it, "Everything you always wanted to know about Jackalopes* but didn't think you oughtta ask." The reference work is written in question and answer style and includes a table of helpful jackalope statistics such as how the population has declined since 1850.

The state travel people appear to feel a caveat regarding the authenticity of the endangered species is in order, because they make it clear to us that "If anyone has still mythed the point, it's a put on!"

If there is snow, you can xc ski from your cabin at Esterbrook. Check with the ranger at the Medicine Bow National Forest work center just down the road for trail information.

At times a local rancher sets tracks for skiers, and he always does so for the February sanctioned xc races. Owners of the lodge, Richard and Ida Mae Stinson, are members of the USSA, northwest ski division.

Though adequate, cabins at the remote areas are either tiny and sparsely furnished or primitive, or both.

Casper area skiers often seek snow at Esterbrook. There is mounting interest in xc skiing in Casper, but both snow conditions and a dearth of designated ski trails have thus far stunted the growth of the activity. Local skiers tend to migrate toward Casper Mountain, 7 miles south. But much of the land there is privately owned and can only be accessed upon the granting of special permission.

Esterbrook Lodge, a local retreat favorite, offers cabins, meals, dancing on Saturday nights and a view of Laramie Peak. The lodge complex of rustic cottages is in a summer cabin area southwest of Douglas, Wyoming.

Hotel Wolf

Location
On Wyoming 130, at Saratoga, 42 miles southeast of Rawlins; 150 miles south of Casper.

Accommodations
17 rooms sleep 1-5 people each. Some private baths. No kitchens. Capacity, 38. Rates start at $7.50 per person in a 2 to 5 person arrangement. Inquire about special winter packages.

Services
Lunch, dinner, served at hotel; bar on premises. All other services within walking distance.

Trails and Snow Conditions
Marked, non-groomed trails on Medicine Bow National Forest in Snowy Range. Trail heads start about 20 miles southeast of Saratoga. Ski on town golf course during any good snow year.

Ski Rentals and Lessons
Rentals available at Medicine Bow Lodge (see separate listing). No lessons. Touring guides may be available at Wolf if future demand makes the service feasible.

Reservations
Deposit needed for busy weekends. MC, Visa. Make advance arrangements for pets.
Hotel Wolf
P.O. Box 1298
Saratoga, WY 82331
(307) 326-5525

Did you ever stop to buy a case of beer and end up purchasing an entire hotel?

Mike Self did. On a "pilgrimage" home to Wyoming on Bicentennial Day — July 4, 1976 — he happened into what was then the Sisson Hotel. Learning it was for sale, he called his good buddy and former University of Wyoming classmate Doug Campbell, in southern California.

The sellers and the buyers were able to put together a deal, and on April 1, 1977, the new partners took occupancy.

When the new team began operation, a sign was discovered posted on the end of the bar which read, "No smoking, no eating, no beverages — by order of our sheriff." They didn't let that stop them.

Meals had not been served in the 1893 vintage hotel since World War II food rationing put an end to the dining room business. Mike and Doug re-instituted the serving of food and restored each room to its original purpose. That meant putting the dining area where the bar was, and putting the bar where the barber shop once had been.

Hotel staff members are selected with care, and that care is especially apparent in their chef choice. Tastefully prepared dinners, served in lovely surroundings, range into the gourmet category. Dinner begins at 5:30 every evening except

Turn of the century Hotel Wolf, in Saratoga, Wyoming, was originally built as a stage line stopover. New owners are restoring the historic building to reflect its beginnings and provide comfort and ambience for guests.

Sunday, when it is moved up to 4 p.m. to accommodate ski tourers heading for home. Lunch specials are offered almost daily.

In its long history, the inn has had only four owners. It was originally built by Fredrick G. Wolf as a stage stop on the Encampment to Walcott Junction line.

After Wolf's death, the next owner, George W. Sisson, renamed it to reflect new ownership. Sisson drowned in 1935 and two years later, the hotel was purchased by J. Earl Moore. After Moore's death in 1947, widow Mary carried on until the dynamic duo arrived.

In addition to re-establishing both food service and name, the current owners stripped paint off woodwork and added a museum-piece bar. Doug's wife Kathy has done a job with beautiful turn of the century decor which includes striped color-coordinated wallpaper, lace panel curtains and custom-made leaded-glass transoms in the public area.

Above: Furnishings at Hotel Wolf conjure up a bit of nostalgia. Below: Hotel owner Doug Campbell presides over food and drink. Inn meals, served during lunch and dinner hours, range into the gourmet category.

The town of Saratoga is extremely proud — and it should be — of its "Hobo Pool." Private donations support the maintenance of the beautiful and clean outdoor hot springs pool at the south end of town. The lighted pool, open 24 hours a day, is free to everyone. Winter water temperatures generally range between 102-108 degrees. Don't miss one of the better hot pools around.

Twenty miles away, in the Snowy Range, you'll find lots of snow and plenty of trails on varied terrain. See the Medicine Bow Lodge listing for descriptive trail information.

Saratoga's city fathers maintain a free outdoor pool fed by natural hot springs. The large concrete plunge features a small rock enclosure for extra-hot soaking. Excellent skiing is in the nearby Snowy Range.

Medicine Bow Lodge

Location
On Wyoming 130, about 20 miles southeast of Saratoga. *Winter access from west only.*

Accommodations
8 log cabins sleep 2-6 people; "retreat house" (dorm) sleeps 12, for a total capacity of 35. No water in cabins in winter, no kitchens. New central bath house has Jacuzzi and sauna. Propane heat in cabins; wood heat in dorm, where sleeping bags are needed. $33 for small cabins, $45 for larger cabin that holds 5 or more. American plan available. Inquire about a group package for dorm.

Services
Dining room at lodge. Gas, groceries, fast food 1½ miles west on highway.

Trails and Snow Conditions
Virtually unlimited mileage on unplowed forest roads. Car shuttles allow some long one-way tour options. Share most trails with snowmobiles. Lodge elevation 8,300 feet.

Ski Rentals and Lessons
Rentals at lodge. No lessons.

Reservations
A week's notice in winter season (December-April); longer for large groups, MC, Visa. Pets discouraged.
Medicine Bow Lodge
Box 752
Saratoga, WY 82331
(307) 326-5439

Summer dude ranch Medicine Bow Lodge is the perfect winter retreat. Log buildings nestle in the conifers far off the highway, snow piled all around. The only clue that a creek flows past is the rustic wood railing on the foot bridge. Wood heat, a rock fireplace and ruffly white muslin curtains in the main lodge provide coziness when it's nippy outdoors.

The resort was built originally as a private lodge, then was opened to the public in 1917. Over the years, the ranch has been handed from owner to owner. Bill and Bettyann Prather arrived two years ago to take over management of the guest accommodations. Bill, originally from Saratoga, is an ordained minister and psychologist-on-sabbatical.

The lodge and cabins are immaculate and well-maintained. It would appear to be the kind of place where the dinner bell is rung and guests are served beef stew and apple pie. But, here is a surprise. Folks drive up from Saratoga or Rawlins (or over the pass on snow machines) for such delectables as filet mignon and shrimp or New York strip and crab legs. And lavish Sunday brunch is a winner, too. The dining room is so popular, it is open to the public just on weekends, and then by reservation only.

For overnight guests, meals are served seven days a week and no reservations are necessary.

You'll need to ski like crazy to work off the huge meals. You'll have an opportu-

There will be no lack of snow for skiers who visit Medicine Bow Lodge on the west slope of 10,847-foot Snowy Range Pass. The southern Wyoming guest ranch offers access to lengthy ski tours.

nity to do so nearby. Loop trails in the area tend to be long . . . anywhere from 12-20 miles.

Trail heads are well-marked, parking turnouts are many, and trails most likely will have been packed by snowmobile. The area toward the top of the pass is popular with machines — they tend to use trails far east of the lodge. During weekdays, hardly anyone is around. Maps and information are readily available at the Saratoga ranger station.

At least two hefty one-way car shuttle tours may pique the interest of those raring-to-go. A one-way run leaves Highway 130 at South French Creek Road, #227. Ski south until you run out of snow, probably in the vicinity of French Creek Campground. North to south is recommended because it's mostly downhill.

A second option is to ski across Snowy Range Pass from snow line to snow line on unplowed Highway 130. The distance is usually about 20 miles. Go from west to east — it will be more down than up — and you may have a tail wind. The unplowed portion of the road starts about 6 miles east of Medicine Bow Lodge, crosses the 10,847-foot summit and ends about 5 miles west of Centennial, near Medicine Bow Downhill Ski Area.

You can ski there, too, if you're still energetic. Cross country trails are marked and groomed at the downhill area. Although most folks who ski on that side of the Snowies are day skiers from Laramie, 27 miles east, there are two places to stay in Centennial. The Friendly Store and Motel, and The Old Corral, both may be contacted at Centennial, WY 82055.

The roomy main lodge at Medicine Bow ranch provides guests with comfortable lounge area with fireplace, game room and cheery dining room. The mountain inn is a popular dinner spot on weekends.

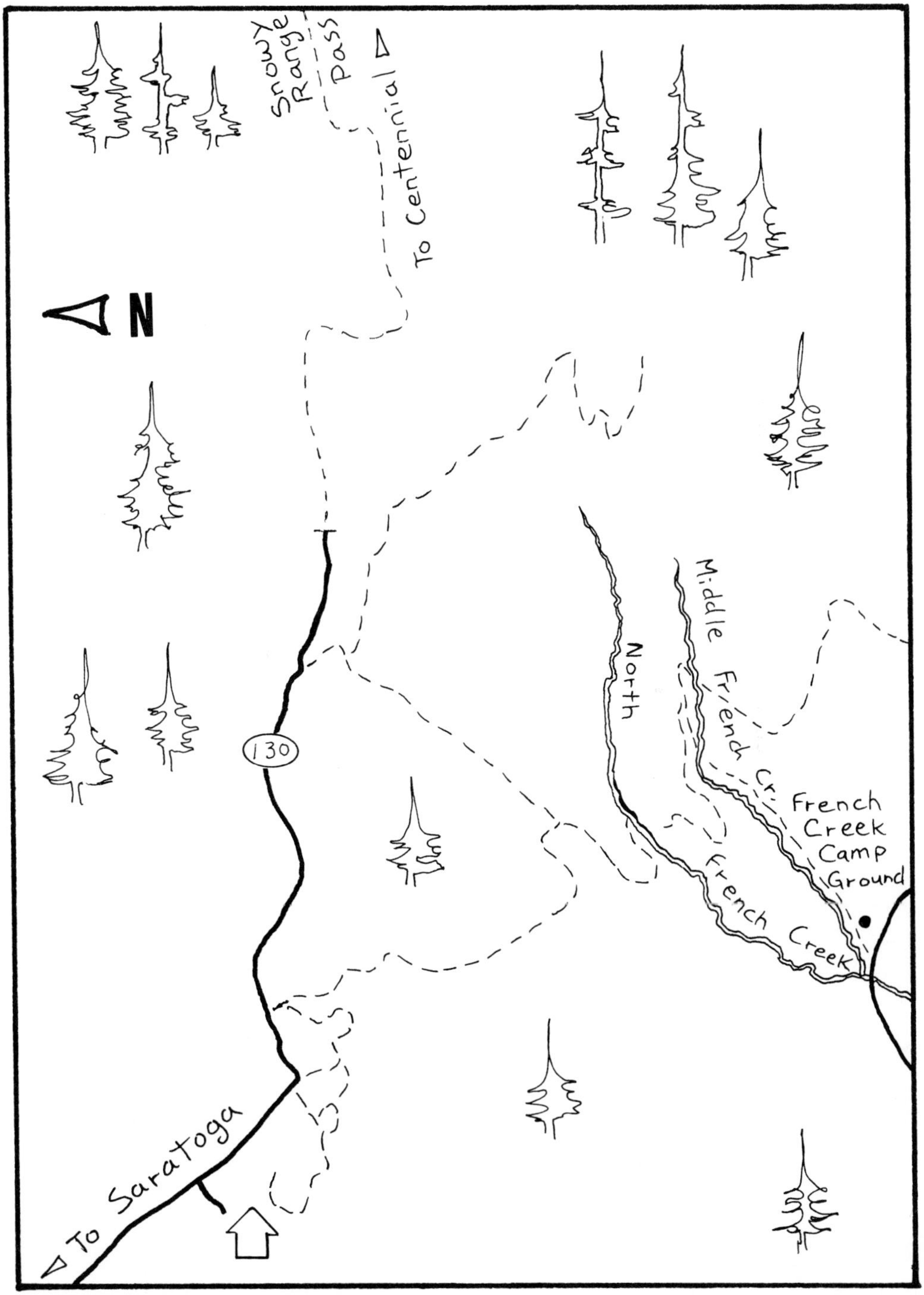

N
Snowy Range Pass
To Centennial
130
North
Middle French Cr.
French Creek Camp Ground
French Creek
To Saratoga

Utah

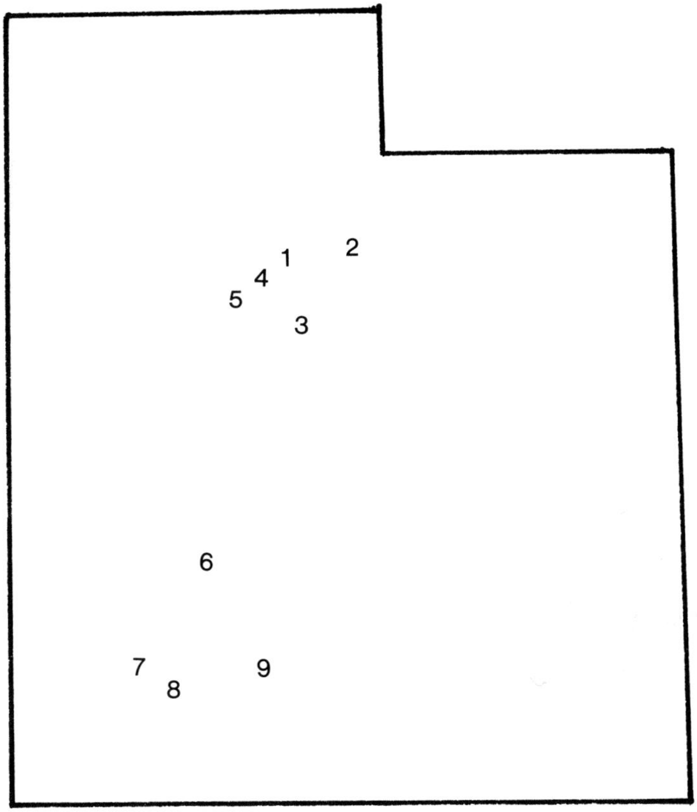

1 Chateau Apres
2 Piute Creek Outfitters
3 The Homestead
4 Silver Fork Lodge
5 Snowpine Lodge
6 Mt. Holly Ski Resort
7 Bristlecone Hostel
8 Meadeau View Lodge
9 Ruby's Inn

Chateau Apres Lodge

Location
In Park City, one block off Utah 224. 20 miles southeast of Salt Lake City.

Accommodations
Private rooms and dorms accommodate 132 people. Rooms have TV, private baths. Two non-coed dorms each sleep 26 in bunks. Sleeping bags not needed. No kitchens. *1982-83* rates start at $33 per night plus tax for 1 or 2 in a room; $9 for a bunk.

Services
Restaurant on premises. All services within walking distance.

Trails and Snow Conditions
White Pine Touring Center maintains 5 kilometers of machine-set tracks at 7,000 feet on city golf course. $1 day fee. Unmarked trails within 10-45 minutes in canyons out of Park City and in the Uinta National Forest. Overnight tours available.

Ski Rentals and Lessons
Rentals and complete instruction, day tour and guide service at White Pine Touring, P.O. Box 417, Park City, UT 84060. (801) 649-8701.

Reservations
By September 1 for Christmas; by December 1 for February and early March.

Chateau Apres Lodge
Box 579
Park City, UT 84060
(801) 649-9372

Park City, Utah, has everything a downhiller's little heart goes pitty-pat for. It has more snow — 40 foot average — than you can shake a ski at.

And it has one of the very few serious Nordic ski touring centers in the state.

Jim Miller and Steve Erickson have achieved a well-deserved reputation for their White Pine Touring Center. The partners have served the needs of xc skiers in the Park City area for ten years and have been at their present location — in the pro shop of the city golf course — for the past eight years.

Their Wasatch Mountains base site provides complete rental, retail and service facilities for xc needs as well as a short flat course for teaching and practice. But that's just the tip of the iceberg.

Above: Old-time mining town Park City, Utah, retains its historic flavor, yet offers upbeat amenities. Below: Chateau Apres provides immediate access to all the town has to offer, including acres of Wasátch snow.

You can participate in a half day "mini-tour", go on an all-day outing into the Uintas, ride the lifts and crank out those telemarks, ski back country, or join the lunch bunch on ladies' day.

A very special option is the High Uintas trip, a tour program under the direction of Steve's sister, Gay Erickson. Three or four weekends a month, groups of three to ten people ski into a summer Boy Scout camp on the East Fork of the Bear River, about 35 miles south of Evanston, Wyoming.

The typical trek starts with a car pool arrangement from Park City on a Friday morning. The 70-mile drive, two or three hours, brings the group to the trail head about noon. The 4 or 5-mile tour into the camp, about 1,000 feet elevation gain along an unplowed road, is the afternoon's ski activity. All-day skiing on Saturday permits the tourer to explore the wonders of the mountains, such as the High Uinta Primitive Area, one mile from the camp, not to mention *fine* Utah powder. A short tour on Sunday morning precedes the return trip to the cars.

One or two guides, depending upon the number of guests, accompany the group. Breakfast and dinner (vegetarian) are provided. Pack your own lunches. Stay in heated but primitive cabins (no water, ski to the john) at 9,000 feet elevation. You don't need to bring a sleeping bag.

This quality program is going into its ninth year of operation. Part of the reason for its success is that the needs and interests of the group dictate the type of touring and level of instruction offered on the trail — and it's fun.

But if several-day, high mountain experience is not you — in the words of Jim Miller, "Park City has over 10,000 beds to choose from." Just off the main drag, Park Avenue, is massive Swiss-style Chateau Apres Lodge, where you are invited to "stay in non-luxurious luxury."

The hotel offers both private rooms and inexpensive dorms and has a relaxed and friendly ambience. The Chateau brochure informs that, "We don't put on airs — we put up skiers."

The middle-of-the-room circular fireplace in the main lounge of the lodge is a cozy place to gather for chit-chat or reading. Wall murals in the upper halls depict the local snow scene, with a south-of-the-border flair. (The artist was espoused to a Spanish lady.)

Busy Chateau Apres Lodge offers both private room and dorm-style accommodations. Nearby White Pine Touring Center, at the city golf course, conducts a well-rounded program of xc activities and services.

The inn dining room is open during breakfast and dinner hours only, but in Park City, every other door on Main Street has a restaurant behind it. The majority of town visitors are on the slopes until 4 p.m. or so, therefore most hotel kitchens simply detour mid-day.

Transportation services in Park City, and from and to Salt Lake, are excellent. Ask the hotel for current schedules.

In spring, Steve and Jim pack up the ski inventory into Jim's old bus and store it away for the summer while golf clubs and sun visors reside in their shop. Jim usually leads Outward Bound programs in the Pacific Northwest while the summer breezes blow. But Steve can't get enough of winter. He goes to avalanche country in New Zealand until the snow flies again in Park City.

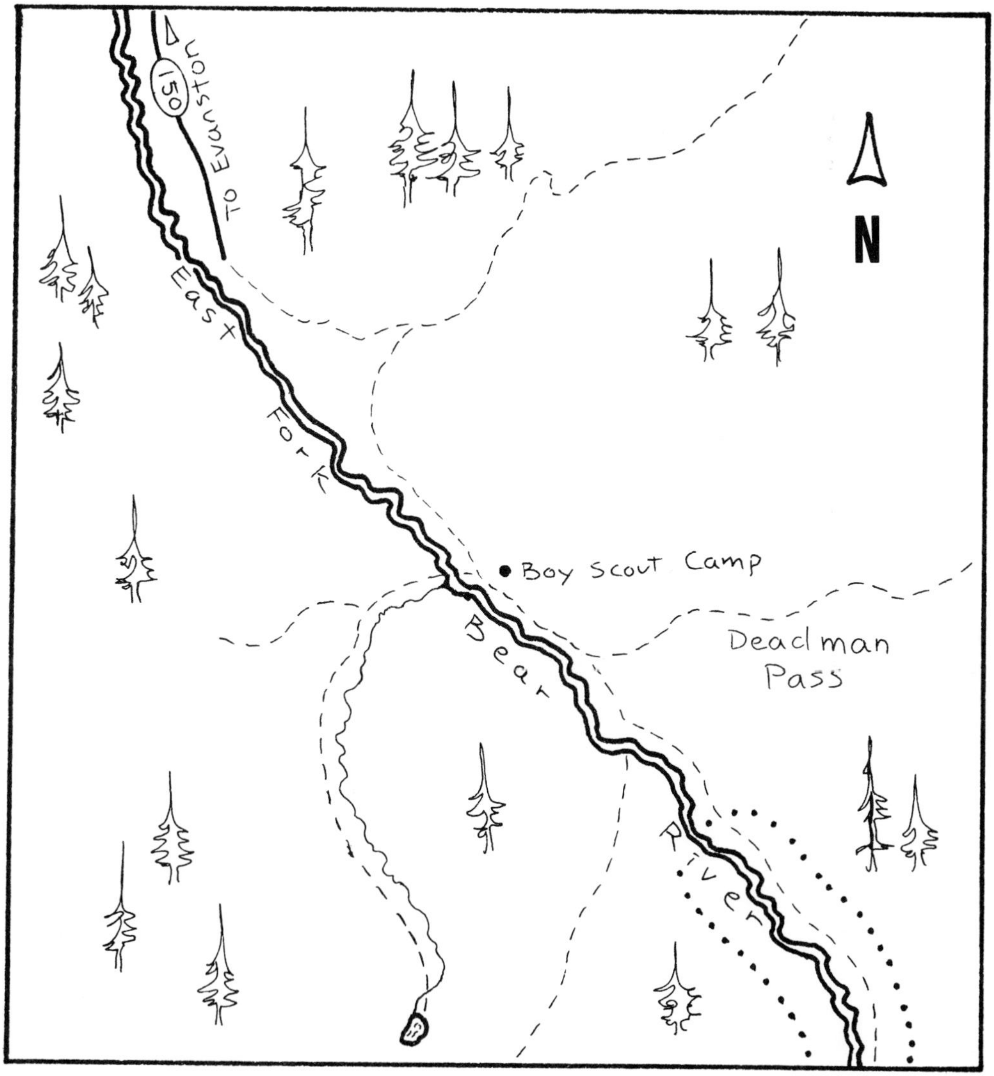

Piute Creek Outfitters

Location
2¾ miles east of Utah 189, at Marion. About 40 miles east of Salt Lake City; 20 miles northeast of Heber. Turn east on "Upper Loop" at Kamas Co-op 3 miles south of Oakley; park at blue and white trailer; *ski in ¾ mile.*

Accommodations
Wrangler bunk house sleeps 8 in bunks, 2 on cots. Wood stove heat. Bedding provided. Plumbing, including hot showers, in cook house. Outdoor privy, no electricity. $50 per night per person includes all meals, instruction and guide service.

Services
Meals served family style. All other services at Kamas, 2 miles south.

Trails and Snow Conditions
Several miles of break-your-own trail touring on unplowed roads and summer horse and hiking trails. All ability levels.

Ski Rentals and Lessons
PSIA certified instructor on premises when guests are present to teach and conduct tours. Rentals at Park City.

Reservations
No credit cards. Pets discouraged.
Piute Creek Outfitters, Inc.
Rt. 1-A
Kamas, UT 84036
(801) 783-4317

Want to go on an "overnight ski party?" That's what Arch and Barbara Arnold call their winter program at Piute Creek Outfitters.

Horse and llama packers by summer and fall, Arch and Barbara open the wranglers' bunk house to xc guests when the snow flies in December. The camp represents a simple, back-to-the-land kind of life. The bunk house (your hotel) has a sod roof and is heated by wood. Though small, it's clean and comfortable.

There's an earth shelter root cellar where food supplies are stored for the winter. Inside temperatures year 'round range between 32 and 52 degrees — perfect for food storage.

A new cook house is light and airy, and water is heated by a combination of solar and wood.

All buildings on the property were constructed by Arch, starting with the Arnolds' cozy cliff-side residence. Arch says it was "built by wrangler labor and ma and pa" during the two-year period 1977-79.

Above: Arch Arnold. Below: Outbuildings and corrals at Piute Creek Outfitters reflect the Arnolds' trail head packer activity for summer vacationers and autumn hunters. The solar cookhouse is at left.

Timber was cut high up in the woods and brought down the hill with horses. The beautiful contemporary-style wood structure has a peeled-log ceiling with natural critter designs on the poles.

"We had a devil of a time getting the engraver beetles to stop engraving," says Arch of the intricate patterns overhead. For months after the logs were in place, little piles of pine sawdust would be found on the dining table each morning.

The camp has its own water supply. The only outside help is provided by Mountain Bell.

The natural life is also reflected in furnishings — Peruvian blankets on the built-in sofa, animal hides on the wall, gas lantern hanging from a nail, fruit leather in a brown pot, and a reed pack basket for carrying in supplies by ski.

Don't misinterpret this scene; Piute Creek (named for the stream you ski across on your way in) is no hippie enclave. It's a chosen way of life for a man who spent 28 years — you'd never guess — as an officer in the U.S. Army. The Arnolds began the outfitting business in 1973 and added the ski touring program in the winter of 1980-81.

In addition to overnight services, skiers may opt for half-day or full-day tours. These outings include a guide and a "hot chili lunch with sourdough bread and tea or cocoa" in the cookhouse social center.

Above: Summer wranglers' bunks are plain but serviceable guest quarters by winter. Below: The Arnolds' hand-hewn residence is on the hill, a partial supply of winter wood at left, and the bunkhouse on the right.

Piute Creek is the only Utah lodge in the winter business exclusively to attract ski tourers.

The unique experience in this charming Uinta Mountains setting will send you back to the city refreshed and reflective. The personalities and philosophy of the owners are special in themselves and the ski touring country is different from that farther west in the Wasatch. An example: there is no avalanche danger!

Arch has identified three trail levels, both skill-wise and geographically, in the area. Going from the ranch up Hoyt Canyon, level 1 follows unused roads along the west face of South Mountain and loops back to camp. The second level, call "Secret Loop," is a 3-3½ hour tour on the north face. You can ski to the mountain top and view 11,750-foot Mt. Timpanogos ("reclining Indian maiden") north of Provo Canyon or loop back to camp.

Level 3, into Paulsin Basin, is a strenuous tour with an elevation gain from 6,800 feet at base camp to 8,500 feet. Typical skiing in this area is short powder bowl runs.

When you visit Piute Creek Outfitters, be prepared for a quiet mountain retreat experience. And know that you will meet some very *special* people.

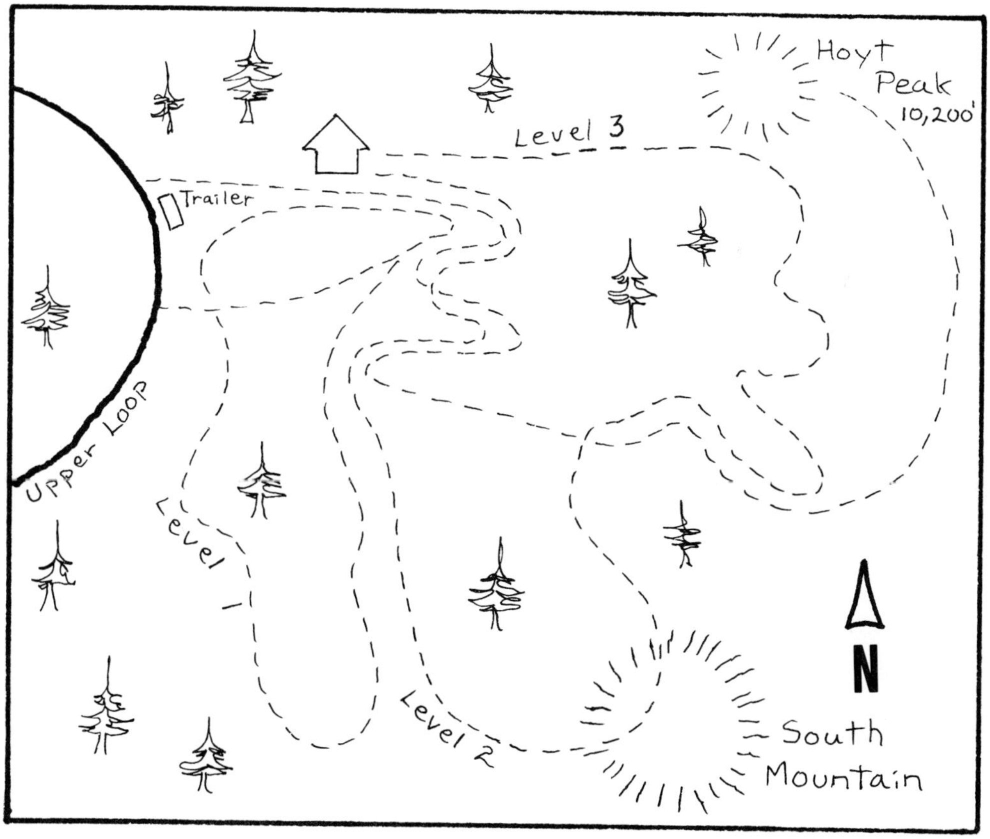

The Homestead

Location
On Homestead Drive, at Midway, Utah. About 4 miles west of Heber; 20 miles south of Park City; 50 miles southeast of Salt Lake City.

Accommodations
43 units, housing 2 to 6 each, accommodate approximately 170 guests. Some TV, some fireplaces. No phones, no kitchens. Conference facilities. Rates start at $36 for two.

Services
Dining room, swimming pool, Jacuzzi, sauna, outdoor hot tub and mineral pool. Swim suit rentals. Other services at Heber.

Trails and Snow Conditions
7 miles of machine-set tracks on public golf course, 1½ miles north of lodge. No snowmobiles permitted on course. Other touring in Daniels Canyon/Strawberry Reservoir area, on U.S. 40, about 20 miles southeast of the Homestead.

Ski Rentals and Lessons
Rentals in Park City. Check with White Pine Touring Center for lesson information (see Chateau Apres listing).

Reservations
Usually need to reserve weekends a month in advance.
The Homestead
700 N. Homestead Drive
Midway, UT 84049
(801) 654-1102
532-2100 in Salt Lake City
377-9149 in Provo

The Homestead offers the Utah tourer a refreshing change of pace.

The lodging represents a fascinating mix of sophistication, relaxation, privacy and elegance. As you drive onto the spacious grounds, you'll see a "Virginia plantation" scene — with two-story structures and tall trees. As you enter the lobby, with its lace window panels and burnished antique wood, you'll begin to feel that the inn promises something much different from your basic winter mountain hut or downhill ski resort madness.

Leaving the main building, a stroll down a park-like path will bring you to your lodgings. Open the door to a room well-furnished with antiques. Some of the guest rooms are original farm buildings. For example, the "Virginia House" was the first farm home, and the "Milk House" was just that.

Though the Homestead is located in the notorious Wasatch Range, you will find ski touring turf as easy to manage as cup-a-soup. At the local golf course, in Wasatch Mountain State Park, set tracks offer a pleasant outing for beginning tourers. Hilly terrain on one portion of the course provides more ski challenge than do most golf links tracks.

The Homestead is close to major ski areas and being down at the 5,600-foot

Utah's Homestead is an early-day farm, the original owner of which gave up on agriculture to open the grounds for visitors seeking relaxation in hot water springs. Some of the first farm buildings now house guests.

level presents no lack-of-snow problem. From Thanksgiving through early March, you can ski from your cottage door. Park City is a half-hour drive from the Homestead and nearby Piute Creek Outfitters (see separate listings) offers yet a different kind of touring.

If you run out of ski terrain (laugh here), a variety of other diversions awaits you at the inn. Horse sleigh rides; an outdoor ice skating pond (bring your own skates); the gamut of hot tubs, mineral pools and swimming facilities all are available in this natural hot spring setting.

Top: The lobby of the main building at The Homestead sets the scene for a serene and peaceful visit. Below: Homestead facilities include two attractive dining areas, antique-filled guest rooms, and indoor and outdoor pools.

An undeveloped hot spring pool may be accessed on Utah 224, just east of the golf course.

The "hot pots" were a force to be dealt with by first land owner, Swiss farmer Simon Schneitter, who found that the copious quantities of bubbling warm water "made his alfalfa soggy!" So many of Simon's friends came to soak in his springs that he finally gave up his frustrating efforts to farm the incorrigible acreage and opened a resort — "Schneitter's Hot Pots", he called it.

Mrs. Schneitter, Fanny, began food service for guests, and her tradition of excellence continues now. The inn dining room serves only at meal hours during winter, so be sure to get there on time to sample such breakfast specialties as huevos rancheros, quiche lorraine and Utah rainbow trout. Dinner delectables may be topped off with the likes of country style pecan pie or deep dish cherry pie.

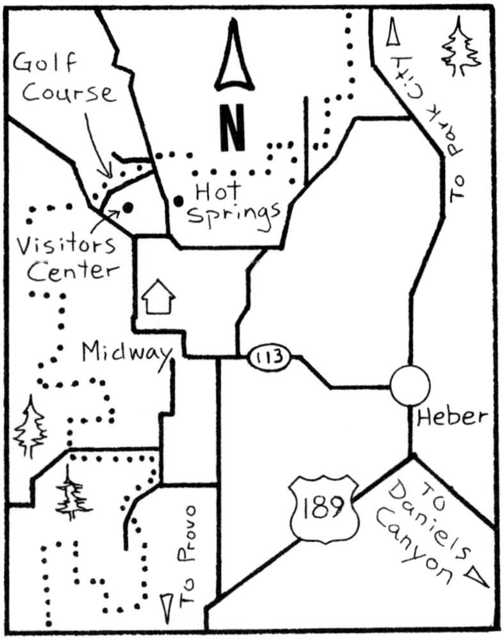

Silver Fork Lodge

Location
On Utah 152, in Big Cottonwood Canyon, 20 miles southeast of downtown Salt Lake City.

Accommodations
8 rooms sleep 2-4 each for a total capacity of 25. Private baths; no kitchens. 2-night minimum. 5-night minimum Christmas and Easter weeks. Doubles start at $35.

Services
Restaurant on premises. Groceries, liquor store at Brighton Village. Gas at Salt Lake City.

Trails and Snow Conditions
15 kilometers of machine-set tracks at Brighton Ski Touring Center. Variety of trail conditions for all ability levels. $3 trail fee. Unlimited break-your-own-trail touring in the more difficult category.

Ski Rentals and Lessons
Complete rentals, instruction and guide service at Brighton Ski Touring Center, Brighton, UT 84121; (801) 649-9156.

Reservations
A week ahead often okay. In fall for Christmas and Easter weeks. MC; Visa. No pets. ($300 fine for dogs in Salt Lake City watershed.)
Silver Fork Lodge
Brighton, UT 84121
(801) 649-9551

In the words of Brigham Young, when he first gazed upon Salt Lake Valley, "This is the place." For the xc tourer looking for a spot to ski in the Wasatch, *this* is the place.

"I'm not afraid to say we have a superior track," declares Brighton Touring Center ski school director, Chris Allaire. "Our track is our bread and butter, we take pride in it and work very hard." Chris indicates that U.S. ski team members, competing at Brighton in last year's Dannon races, stated the area is as good or better than Telemark, Wisconsin.

Citizen racers have an opportunity to zoom around the beautifully groomed course six times during each winter's race season series.

Brighton Touring Center partners Dave Carter and Don Despain are in their fifth season of operation in Big Cottonwood Canyon. They established the center in response to a forest service stated need for something besides downhill skiing on land designated as multi-use. Tourers craved a place to go — previously only the hottest of shots could perambulate the near-vertical hillsides surrounding Salt Lake City. And, like Colorado, the Wasatch Range is very popular with avalanches.

Tourers who wish to use the local lifts and downhill slopes may do so, but are required to use safety straps here as well as at most Utah resorts.

The Wasatch is the most heavily-used national forest in the United States, according to Silver Fork Lodge operators Avis and Jim Light. Winter and summer, 1½ million visitors trek up Big Cottonwood Canyon alone. Avis says that ski

Behind Silver Fork Lodge, visitors will discover immediate access to excellent skiing. Snow in the Big Cottonwood Canyon location is abundant and usually accompanied by sunshine. Set tracks and forest trails are available.

tourers in the area like to ski off-trail as well as at Brighton's tracks, "depending on how advanced or crazy they are." She cautions that touring off trail in the settled areas of the canyon must be done with care. Power lines running from cabin to cabin often are waist or neck high when approached from the top of snow pack and sometimes live wires are hidden just under the surface of deep snow.

The canyon is a 19th century mining area and abandoned mine shafts present a special danger when openings are concealed by snow. The mining town of Silver Fork flourished just south of the site of the present lodgings.

Silver Fork Lodge was built as a store and cafe shortly after World War II. Rooms for overnight guests were added about 25 years ago. Jim and Avis have owned the facilities about 15 years.

Avis is from Pennsylvania and brings recipes with her, including Pennsylvania Dutch Shoo-Fly pie, a *rich* concoction of molasses, brown sugar and cinnamon, topped with a crumb crust. She also bakes such hard-to-find yummies as elderberry pie.

Jim's specialty is sourdough pancakes and they are so popular, he can hardly keep enough starter brewing.

Above: The entrance to groomed trails at Brighton Ski Touring Center leads to a wonderland of terrain choices. Below: The Nordic center at Brighton Village offers services and goods for touring needs.

In an annual "best and worst" issue, Utah Magazine rated Silver Fork Lodge in a three-way tie for best pancakes. The publication also named it "Best eating place in Big Cottonwood Canyon."

The clean and cozy lodge kitchen does have some competition in the canyon. At Brighton, the Village Store houses upstairs gourmet dinner restaurant, the Blind Miner, open Thursday through Saturday — reservations suggested. The eatery was named for Roy Newman, a local miner who, at age 35, was blinded by a mining-related explosives accident. Despite his impairment, Roy was able to perform the engineering function of blasting straight and perfect tunnels, up until his death in 1974 — at age 80.

The touring center schedules moonlight tours topped off by a gourmet dinner at the Blind Miner.

Other diversions may be found in the area. Molly Green's Pub at Mt. Majestic Manor is a favorite social center at the end of the canyon. Ms. Green was a turn of the century resident who ran the local sawmill and provided laundry services for the miners.

Back at Silver Fork, you'll be cozy and warm in your lodge room. Open the inside wood shutters for a beautiful view across the canyon. Those names over the room doors — Navajo Night, Yellowstone, Wheat — don't refer to Western lore. They are the names of wood stain used on the pine paneling inside. Each of the guest rooms is a slightly different tone, stained and labeled with care by a previous owner.

The same TLC is applied today (although not with a paint brush) by the Lights.

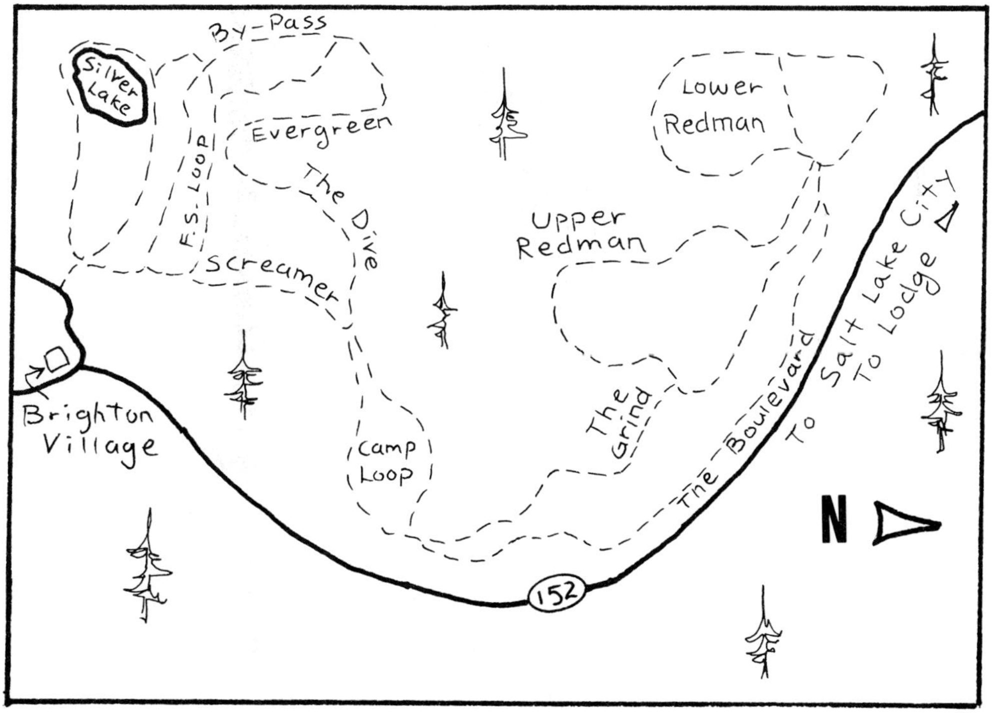

Snowpine Lodge

Location
On Utah 210, in Little Cottonwood Canyon, at Alta; 25 miles southeast of Salt Lake City.

Accommodations
Dorm style, 4-to-a-room arrangements, with bath down the hall. No kitchens. $30 per night includes breakfast and dinner.

Services
Restaurant, game room on premises. Most other services in area.

Trails and Snow Conditions
Break your own trail over the ridges; or ride the Alpine lifts and ski in Albion Basin. Ski to Park City, 12 miles; Brighton, 3. This is for the *heaviest* duty skier. Base elevation, 8,700 feet.

Ski Rentals and Lessons
Rentals, lessons, tours, guide service available at lodge. Complete ski shop on premises.

Reservations
MC, Visa.
Snowpine Lodge
Alta, UT 84092
(801) 742-3274

Alta is an outrageous area for downhillers. Vertical, one might say. So it's not every tourer's cup of tea.

Some think it advisable to use bubble gum klister to scale that first canyon wall.

Snowpine Lodge's Al Kapp assures us that "There is plenty of cross country and touring area here. Access by lifts, and/or walking (on skis)."

If you know the way, you can ski 3 miles north to Brighton in Big Cottonwood Canyon, the next crevasse over. Once there you can glide along on meticulously manicured trails. But watch out for the abandoned mine shafts on the way.

The tour to Park City, about 12 miles, is downhill all the way — after you first-gear it over the summit. Get a guide to go with you. And be in great shape.

There is so much vertical real estate in the Wasatch Mountains that the traditional mode of ascent is via mechanical lift. A new breed of Nordic nut is evolving that has learned to overcome this artificial aid. These kamikazes are able to ski down groomed Alpine slopes, with or without benefit of telemark. All this downhilling activity has been ripping out pin bindings to such an extent that a Salt Lake City tourer has developed a binding — the Voile — especially designed to ensure the longevity of toe plates.

If you like this kind of athletic suffering, you'll love Alta. And you'll probably really go for Snowpine. The crowd there is young, and the friendliest in Utah. They're all having a good time — and so will you.

An excellent public transportation system from Salt Lake City makes life just a little bit easier for Wasatch skiers frequenting Big and Little Cottonwood Canyons. Plenty of snow and steep terrain are features at Alta.

Atmosphere at Snowpine is more reminiscent of a college dorm than a ski lodge. Accommodations provide four single beds to a room — clothes strewn hither and yon. The central eating area has a cafeteria-style snack bar and serves as a gathering place for exuberant skiers, most of them downhillers.

The lodge, originally dubbed the "Rock Shelter," was constructed by the forest service in the late '30's. After an avalanche distroyed part of the building, a special slab roof was placed upon the structure to avoid future hazard.

Descend into the lodge from the road, straight down a stairway shaft which resembles a long mine tunnel. The image

Above: The first descent at Snowpine Lodge is not accessed by ski lift, but immediately from the highway. Below: Former forest service rock shelter, Alta's Snowpine now offers food, lodging and complete ski services.

it conjures up is fitting, because tiny Alta was the center of a silver mining area which boomed in 1872. At that time the local population was 5,000.

Some of the early residents hopped onto their skis of a Saturday night to see what was happening on the other side of the mountain.

Today's public transportation schedules from Salt Lake to Little Cottonwood Canyon read like a commuter's timetable. Frequent bus runs are routed regularly from both downtown and the airport. Call (801) 263-3737 for bus information.

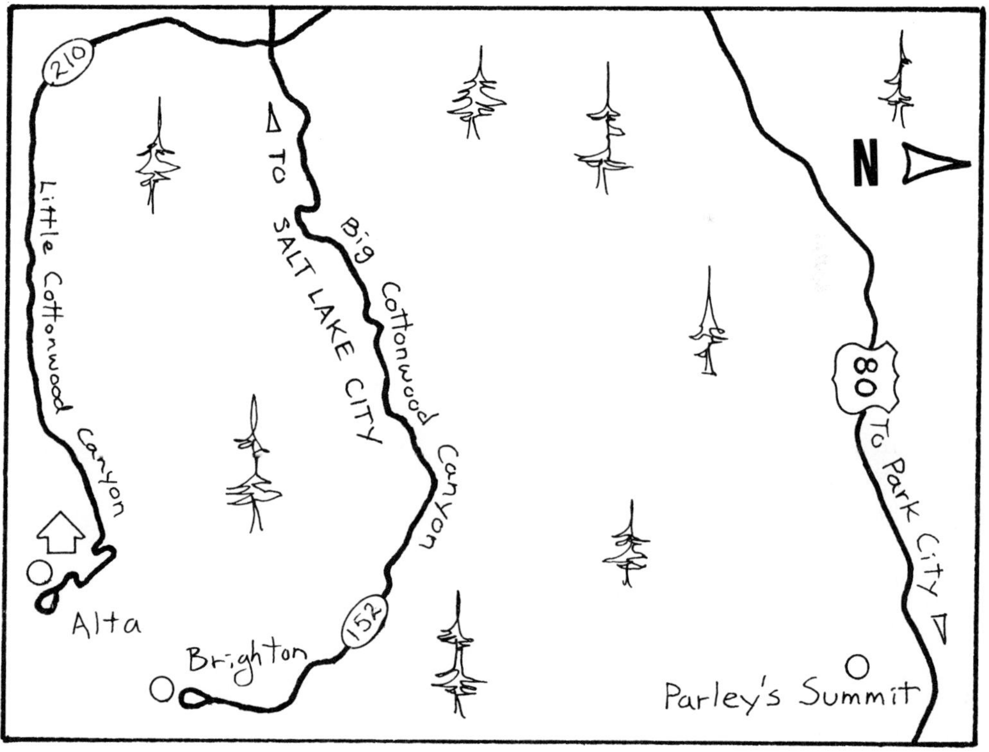

Mt. Holly Ski Resort

Location
On Utah 153, 17 miles east of Beaver; 106 miles northeast of Cedar City. *Winter access from west only.*

Accommodations
57 condos sleep up to 10 people each; 22 motel units house 2-4. Modern 2 and 3-story condos feature lofts, fireplaces and/or wood stoves, kitchens. Condos $65-90 per night. Motel rooms $25 and $35, weekdays; $35 to $45 weekends. Inquire about group rates and special packages.

Services
Restaurant, beer pub, game room on premises. Gas, groceries at Beaver.

Trails and Snow Conditions
Ski from door on unplowed road 2 miles to 9,655-foot Puffer Lake, farther if packed by snowmobiles. Meadow terrain for touring 4 miles below Mt. Holly. Ride lift to 10,200-foot top if you're a dynamite skinny skier.

Ski Rentals and Lessons
Rentals at resort ski shop. No xc lessons.

Reservations
2 weeks for most winter weekends; 6 weeks for holidays. MC, Visa. No pets.

Mt. Holly Ski Resort
P.O. Box 729
Beaver, UT 84713
(801) 438-5030

Want to explore some new turf? Get away from the masses? Experience Utah powder and crystal blue skies? Maybe have access to an uncrowded Alpine slope?

You can get it all at barely-discovered Mt. Holly Resort in southern Utah.

Californians are just beginning to find Mt. Holly and, at present, they constitute the bulk of Holly's market. The area is so fresh that the most elderly condos are only four years old.

Accommodations border on luxurious. Most units have a view of the mountains, and . . . the snow is likely to be up around your window sills. Drop bread crumbs when walking or driving to the main lodge. You won't be able to see over the top of the snow to determine which alley of the maze you're in.

A nice little plus is daily "snow shuttle" service available to the resort from Beaver, Milford or Parowan airports. Call (801) 438-2654 or 438-2659 for information and reservations.

The Mt. Holly people indicate that the area "has made skiing fun again — the way it used to be when there was a lot more mountain than there were skiers."

It's true. This gorgeous spot is an ideal choice for the skier who likes both Alpine and Nordic or for the downhiller converting to touring.

Mountain pocket ski resort Mt. Holly, in Southern Utah, offers pristine touring conditions and uncrowded slopes. Both motel rooms and contemporary condominiums are available for overnight guests.

Bristlecone Hostel

Location

On Utah 143, 1 mile south of Brian Head Village, ½ mile north of Cedar Breaks National Monument. 15 miles south of Parowan; 175 miles north of Las Vegas. *Winter access from Parowan or Panguitch Lake only.*

Accommodations

4 rooms sleep about 4 each for a comfortable capacity of 15. The 2-story hostel has kitchen and living room with fireplace. Sleeping bag and towels needed. Share space with strangers or bring your gang and rent the whole cabin. Overflow lodging available for large groups. Basic weekday rate, $25 for two; $27 on weekend. Entire cabin rents for $102 weekdays and $112 per night on the weekend.

Services

Jacuzzi on premises. All services except gas available at village. Gas at Parowan.

Trails and Snow Conditions

5 kilometers set tracks near hostel — $1 day fee. Unlimited plateau skiing along rim of Breaks. Back country tours available.
Ski the downhill slopes. Elevation at tracks, 9,900 feet.

Ski Rentals and Lessons

Rentals and complete instruction and guide service at Brian Head Nordic at the village. Box 30, Brian Head, UT 84719
(801) 677-2012.

Reservations

Bristlecone Hostel
P.O. Box 95
Brian Head, UT 84719
(801) 677-2059

Cedar Breaks National Monument *has* to be Utah's big secret.

The nine-mile-wide amphitheater boasts the most subtle and delicate pinks and corals as may be found at Bryce and it's in a small enough area to be comprehensible. Sunsets on the west-facing cliffs and against nearby 11,400-foot Brian Head Peak glow lavender on the glittering evening snow.

One may ski for miles along the relatively flat plateau characteristic of the Breaks rim and take in the beauty of the rugged 2,000-foot deep bowl all along the way.

Although the wind may whip up from time to time, it's likely that the sun will warm you, the sky will be *blue* and the snow may never melt. Cedar Breaks' summit is 10,400 feet and it is not unusual for the road to remain unplowed until the end of May. Drifts often peak at 20-30 feet. Ski access to this magnificient plateau may be made from either end, but accommodations are to be found near Brian Head Ski Resort to the north.

Bristlecone, not really a hostel but a rather funky "cabin" near the Monument, is somewhat removed physically and spiritually from the bustle of the downhill area. Walk in over the snow about 150 yards to the hostel from where you park your car. You can ski out the door to the wonders of the Breaks and to a small, groomed flat-track area maintained by Brian Head Nordic Ski Shop.

The "hostel" is more suitable for groups than for individual use. It's small — one might even say intimate (or crowded). Two of the rooms are under-the-eaves type affairs; big folks must take care for the tops of their heads.

Bring your sleeping bag and sleep on a mattress on the floor. Share a small kitchen (two refrigerators) with other guests.

The pink and coral rocks of amphitheater Cedar Breaks accent the scenery along the 10,400-foot elevation rim plateau. Unlimited touring in the sparsely-wooded area ranges from level terrain to a climb up Brian Head Peak.

Although the hostel is relatively isolated from the more expensive village condos and the lifts of the Alpinists, it's a short drive to the Brian Head post office and the village social center. The Bear Flat Saloon has live music on weekends. Ferdinand's, one of two good restaurants, specializes in Mexican food and steaks. Be prepared for *hearty* portions. Sunday brunch at Ferdinand's features such temptations as quiche reales and crepes y pollo.

Also at the village you'll find Brian Head Nordic, established five years ago by Bill Morris. Bill operates a complete xc service — instruction, guides, rentals — but the program is in a state of transition at present. In the past, the Nordic Center operated the hostel. Now Bill, who splits his time between the ski service and a faculty position at Southern Utah State College, dreams of making the Brian Head plateau area *"the* place in the U.S. to do extensive ski touring," but finds his plans a bit in limbo. His staff is available for several-day back country tours of 15-25 miles per day, but his planned "hut to hut," overnight aspect of the program is uncertain at this time.

If you are interested in covering a lot of trail distance in a magnificent avalanche-free touring area, give Bill a call. He can custom-tailor a great trip for you.

Scheduled Nordic events throughout the season include moonlight tours, ski-joring, xc races and after-ski parties.

Bristlecone Hostel, near Brian Head Ski Resort in Southern Utah, provides the tourer proximity to both groomed trails and the vast expanse of the Cedar Breaks plateau. Overnight guide service is available locally.

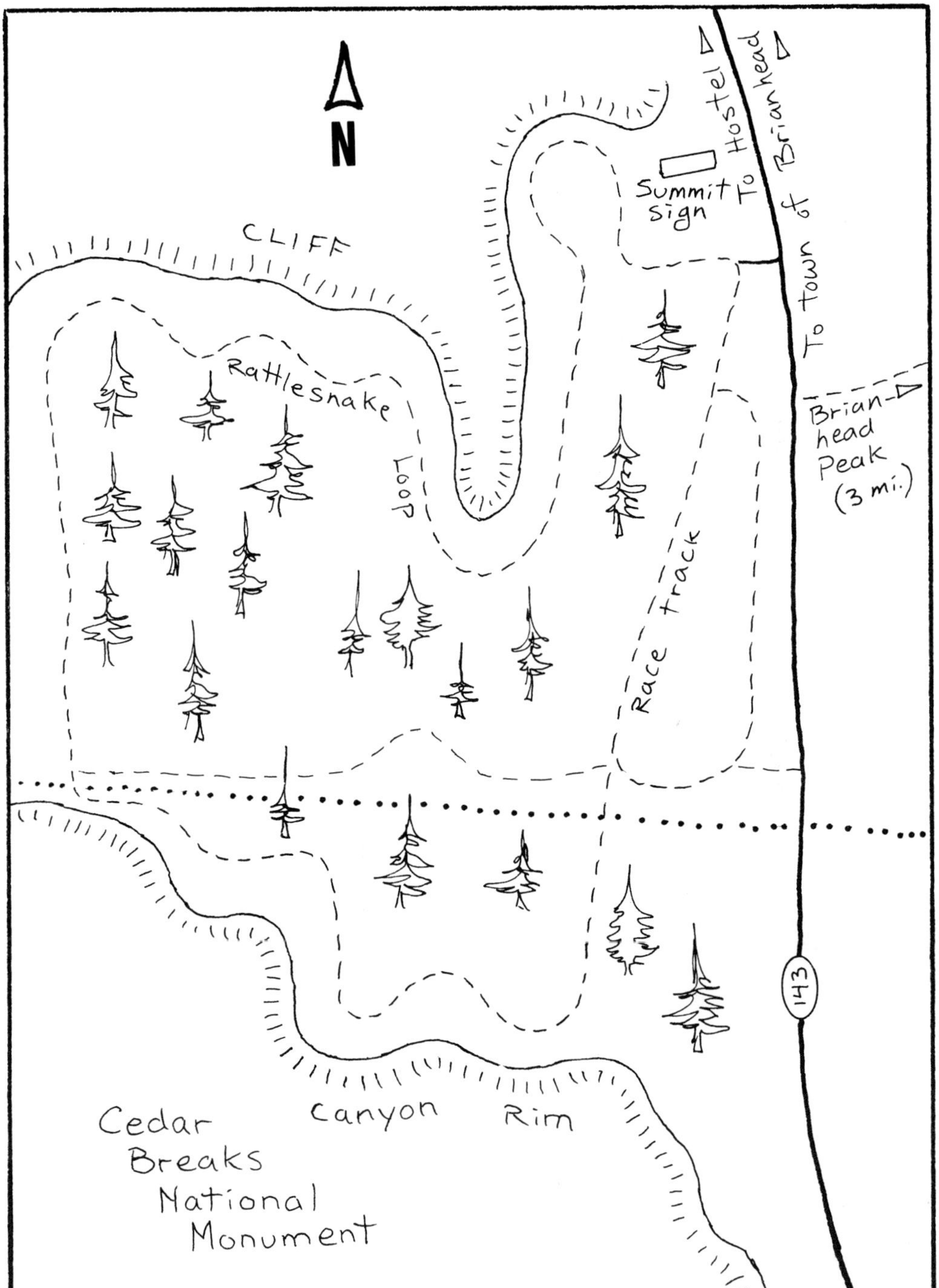
N
CLIFF
Summit sign
To Hostel
To town of Brianhead
Rattlesnake
Loop
Race track
Brian-head Peak (3 mi.)
143
Cedar Breaks National Monument
Canyon Rim

Meadeau View Lodge

Location
On Utah 14, at Duck Creek Village, 30 miles east of Cedar City; 11 miles west of U.S. 89 junction. Although Highway 14 from Cedar City may be closed during or after a winter storm, the approach from U.S. 89 east of Duck Creek is open year around.

Accommodations
9 rooms with private baths sleep 2-5 people each. Lodge capacity, 24. $34 per night includes continental breakfast. Deluxe rooms, $44. $8 each additional person.

Services
Restaurant, beer bar at village. All other services, 30 miles away.

Trails and Snow Conditions
Ski from door on machine-set tracks in adjacent meadow or on infinite variety of unmarked trails in area.

Ski Rentals and Lessons
Complete rentals, instruction and guide service available from Cornice Crashers Ski Tours. Make arrangements with lodge.

Reservations
Two weeks for weekends advisable; longer for holidays. No credit cards. No pets.
Meadeau View Lodge
P.O. Box 356
Cedar City, UT 84720
(801) 648-2495

This is ski touring the way it used to be . . . before flat-track all-stars; pre cross country downhill.

The latter styles are available to you at Meadeau View, but the biggest attraction is the kind of quiet, gentle terrain so difficult to find elsewhere in Utah. And, you don't have to sacrifice one iota of snow quality, sunshine or outrageous scenery to get it.

You'll find snow at this 8,400-foot location long after winter has abandoned most other areas. Spring skiing is fantastic. At Meadeau View, the wind seldom blows and the snow is eight feet deep.

Ski from your door to Aspen-Mirror Lake, over meadows and through aspens along the creek. Or, tour a magnificent 10-mile round trip to Zion Overlook — one of the most breath-taking panoramic lunch stops a xc skier can hope for.

After a morning of glorious skiing through winter-bare aspens and along expansive meadows, a cliff-top lunch stop is a welcome break. The panorama from Zion Overlook includes a glimpse of the distant Zion canyon rim.

Lodge proprietors Harry and Gaby Moyer will arrange a car drop-off for you if you'd like a tour that will provide a downhill run all the way back to the lodge. They might also be persuaded to go along on a loop tour where you stop at a cabin at lunch time.

If you feel the need to venture farther, southern Utah is one big rainbow playground. Meadeau View is within easy driving distance of Brian Head, Bryce Canyon and Cedar Breaks National Monument. (Don't miss this one — nobody outside Utah has heard of it, but its winter beauty rivals Bryce and Zion.) See separate listings for trail descriptions.

Snowmobiles are practically unheard of here. They're not restricted, and occasionally you will see them on weekends, but they don't travel in swarms. Chances are, you'll welcome their packed trail.

Flat tracks await you both in the meadow near the lodge and at Brian Head Nordic.

Many Utah xc skiers are converted downhillers. A lot of them are ambidexterous — Alpine-footed and Nordic-footed at the same time. They're inventing a sport some refer to as Norpine. It means skiing everywhere on anything — with only your toes hooked down.

Bill Murphy of Cornice Crashers Ski Tours serves the ski needs of Meadeau View guests. He's one of the all purpose skiers, and he describes some of the scary stuff as "three pin thrills." Although Bill instructs first-time skiers as well as

Left: Meadeau View's fireplace provides a snug spot to swap ski stories. Above: Host Gaby and Harry Moyer, left, make Duck Creek a return-visit must. Below: The year 'round lodge is easily accessed by highway.

seasoned ones, if what you want is jumping off ledges or riding avalanches, he's your man.

Another important feature you won't have to sacrifice to ski at Meadeau View is quality lodging. Homey rooms are modern, clean, carpeted, cheery, pine-paneled and — are you ready? — beds are equipped with *electric blankets!* Deluxe rooms are spacious — almost elegant. Some rooms have outside entrances.

The charm of the log lodge is evident the moment you step into the main room, which is dominated by a large central circular fireplace. But the warmth merely *begins* here.

The true personality of the lodge lies in the charisma of Gaby and Harry. It's like being a guest in the home of a friend. They're at Duck Creek because it's where they want to be. Retired insurance broker Harry and former teacher Gaby, left Los Angeles in May 1977 to take over ownership of the lodge which had already captured their hearts.

They had stumbled onto the Cedar City area years before while traveling to Alta for holiday skiing. They made a decision to eventually retire in this part of southern Utah and . . . they did!

Guests are served continental breakfast (Don't let the title fool you. They slip in a little bit more than coffee and sticky bun) and lodge guests may make reservations for dinner.

If you seek a change of menu, the Thunder Inn next door is open from nine to nine. Check in advance, however. The owners sometimes get cabin fever and need to break away for a day or two. And, for evening entertainment, there's a beer bar at the "other end of town." Ski or walk — town is two blocks long.

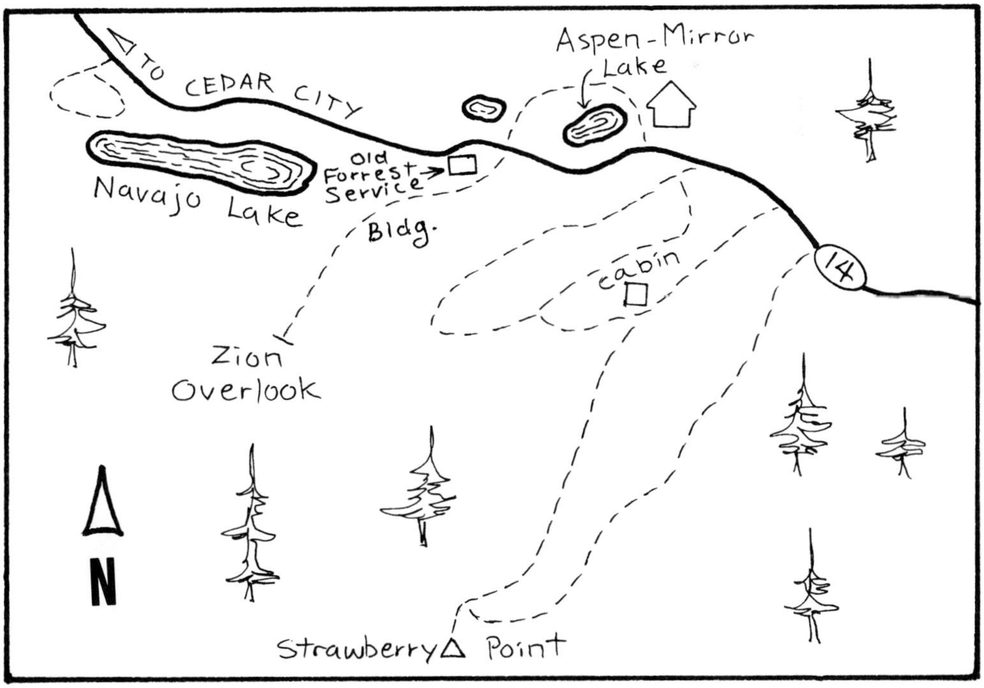

Ruby's Inn

Location
On Utah 63, 1 mile north of Bryce Canyon National Park; 85 miles east of Cedar City.

Accommodations
137 rooms, 2 with kitchens. Bring your own dishes. Private baths, color TV, phones. Most rooms sleep 4. Winter rate, $27 plus tax for two.

Services
Restaurant, laundromat, swimming pool, post office, gas, gift shop on premises. Square dancing on Wednesday nights. Groceries 2 miles. Canyon flights available.

Trails and Snow Conditions
Ski along canyon rim on summer trails. Snow conditions unpredictable and usually no skiing until after January 1. Average annual snowfall, 100 inches.

Ski Rentals and Lessons
No lessons. Nearest rentals, Brian Head Village or Meadeau View Lodge.

Reservations
AM/EX, MC, Visa. Pets are not permitted on park trails or in public buildings.
Ruby's Inn
Ruby's Inn, UT 84764
(801) 834-5341
Toll free in U.S. (800) 528-1234
Toll free in Arizona (800) 352-1222
In Phoenix 257-0885

Like most of nature's wonders, richly-rouged Bryce Canyon is absolutely stunning draped in a fresh blanket of white winter snow.

A trail along the canyon rim provides proximity to a wonderland of incomparable scenes — ruggedly carved pillars of reds, oranges, coral, lavender, ivory and rust fill the "canyon" floor and walls with an array of shapes and sizes. The dark green of an occasional conifer and the crispness of the white snow accentuate erosion's sculpting, and tinting artistry by iron and manganese.

You can ski for several miles along the unplowed road south from the Inspiration Point turnoff (share this route with snowmobiles on weekends) for open-country style touring with limited canyon scenics. Or you can do an easy tour into Fairyland View which is a flat 2-mile round trip offering a magnificient vista.

The rim trail is a favorite with skiers. A one-way tour option along this route starts at Fairyland View and runs 5½ miles to Bryce Point. Elevation along the rim in this area is from about 8,000 to 8,200 feet. Winter vehicle access may be made to Sunrise, Sunset, Inspiration and Bryce Points and Paria View.

Advanced skiers may choose to venture down into the canyon on designated trails. These are steep, fraught with switchbacks and should be approached with an abundance of skill and forethought.

Even in spring when ski conditions can be *quite* marginal, the effort to tour in this incredible area is rewarding. Pack along

Summer visitor-stop Bryce Canyon, in scenic Southern Utah, is a winter treat for ski tourers. Level rim trails and steep canyon descents are touring choices. Snow accentuates the wild colors of the canyon.

your lunch and bask in the mid-day sun at Fairyland View. Skies are blue and cliffs are pink.

A not-to-be-missed treat starts at about 6:30 a.m. when the birds call and the sun rises over the canyon. Drive to any of the open viewpoints — Bryce, Sunrise, and Sunset are especially panoramic.

All winter users should check at the Park Visitors' Center, open 8-4:30, regarding snow, weather and trail conditions.

The Visitors' Center has a winter program which includes guided snowshoe walks and the lending of snowshoes. Information may be obtained from Superintendent, Bryce Canyon National Park, Bryce Canyon, UT 84717; (801) 834-5322.

Bryce is not a canyon per se, but a water-eroded portion of the limestone Wasatch Formation. Although the canyon was named for Ebenezer Bryce, who ran cattle in the Paria Valley in the 1870's, the Paiutes had a much more poetic and colorful title for the phenomenon — Unka-timpe-wa-wince-pock-ich, which means "red rocks standing like men in a bowl-shaped canyon."

Ebenezer's summation of the area was that it's "a hell of a place to lose a cow!"

The indescribable forms have been described by such comparisons as "Queen Victoria;" "a squirrel looking at me;" a squirrel looking the other way," and "platoons of Turkish soldiers in pantaloons." The park brochure depicts winters in Bryce as "frosted and flaming." Apt to the nth degree.

Founder of Ruby's Inn, Reuben Syrett, lent a bit of history to the area himself. In 1916, Ruby and his wife, Minnie, both

Ruby's Inn, nearest winter accommodations to Bryce Canyon National Park, provides visitor services year around. They include canyon flights, square dancing, laundromat, swimming pool. The Park Visitors' Center is open daily.

descended of Morman pioneers, settled on a ranch on the site of what now houses Ruby's "Best Western Motel". Their first glimpse of the spectacular canyon prompted them to request permission of the state to develop a tourist facility along the rim. They opened "Tourist Rest" in 1919 on the present site of Bryce Canyon Lodge.

In 1923, when Bryce was designated a national monument, the Syretts moved the guest accommodations north to the ranch area and changed the name to Ruby's Inn. The canyon was given National Park status in 1928.

In 1926, Minnie's bricklayer papa, H.G. Excell, constructed the massive rock fireplace in the guest lodge. Although Ruby's today is primarily an ultra-modern facility, the portion of the original lodge which houses the fireplace is intact.

Excell, from Kent, England, migrated to Utah with Mormans in 1883. He built the fire opening eight feet wide in front, and above the hearth he laid a steel horizontal panel which came off the first mail truck between nearby Panguitch and Marysvale.

The inscription imbedded into the face of the fireplace, "Tell your friends about me," is composed of petrified wood and bird bones. And probably some rattlesnake teeth, too.

From the look of it, Minnie's daddy was a busy man. Of the residences in Panguitch today. most are old and brick.

A portion of Ruby's antiquated bill of fare still has a place on the updated menu. It includes such items as "meat sandwich, 15¢; served on plate at table, 25¢; bed for one person, $1.25; Bed, 2 in same bed $2.00; ¼ pie, 10¢; whole pie 40¢."

Ruby's son, Carl, and his family today carry on the old host's tradition of hospitality at the closest winter lodging to Bryce Canyon National Park.

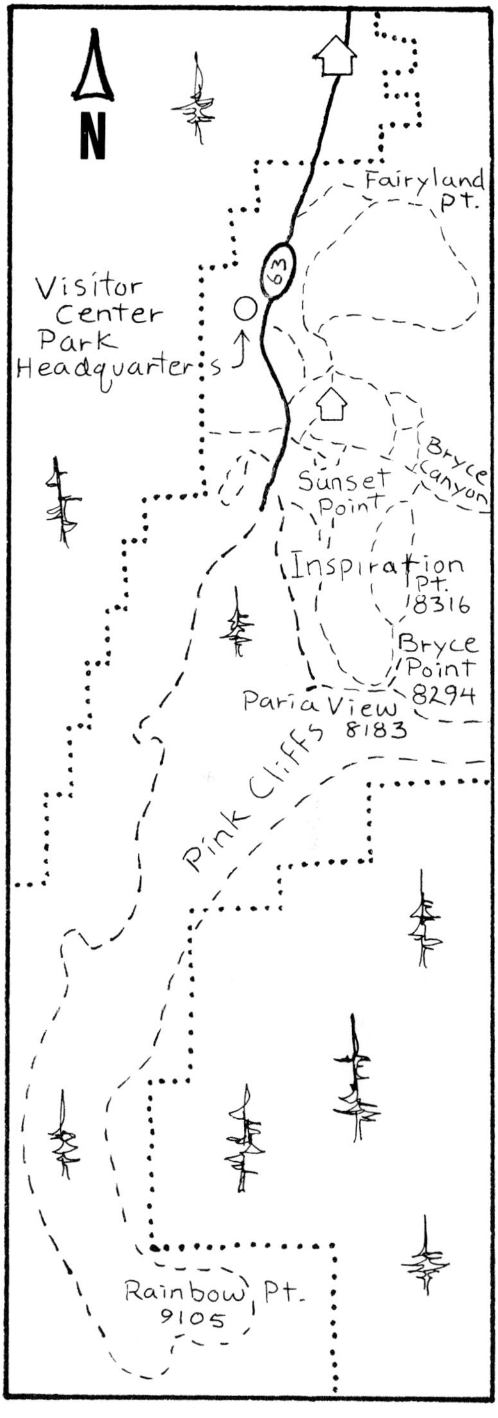

Recommended References

Nordic Skier's Guide to Montana
Elaine Sedlack
Falcon Press Publishing Co., Inc.
P.O. Box 279
Billings, MT 59103

Skiing in Utah — A History
Alexis Kelner
1201 First Avenue
Salt Lake City, UT 84103

Wasatch Tours
Alexis Kelner and David Hanscom
Wasatch Publishers, Inc.
4647 Idlewild Road
Salt Lake City, UT 84117

Yellowstone Nordic Trails
John Barber
(available at the Park)

Trail and Snow Condition Information

Montana

Ski conditions, area information

In-state (406) 449-2654
Out of state (800) 548-3390

Road conditions

Statewide
In-state
(800) 332-6171
Out of state
(406) 449-2675

Within 100-mile radius of:
Billings
(406) 252-2806
Bozeman
(406) 586-1313
Butte
(406) 494-3666
Great Falls
(406) 453-2231
Helena
(406) 449-2641
Kalispell
(406) 755-4949
Missoula
(406) 728-8553

U.S. Forest Service

Beaverhead National Forest

District Ranger
Dillon, MT 59725
(406) 683-2312

District Ranger
Wisdom, MT 59761
(406) 689-2331

Bitterroot National Forest

District Ranger
Sula, MT 59871
(406) 821-3201

District Ranger
Darby, MT 59829
(406) 821-3236

Deerlodge National Forest

District Ranger
Philipsburg, MT 59858
(406) 839-3211

District Ranger
Deer Lodge, MT 59722
(406) 846-1770

Flathead National Forest

District Ranger
Hungry Horse, MT 59919
(406) 387-5243

District Ranger
Whitefish, MT 59937
(406) 862-2508

District Ranger
Columbia Falls, MT 59912
(406) 892-4372

Gallatin National Forest

District Ranger
Big Timber, MT 59011
(406) 932-2650

District Ranger
Gardiner, MT 59030
(406) 848-7231

District Ranger
Bozeman, MT 59715
(406) 587-5271

District Ranger
West Yellowstone, MT 59758
(406) 646-7369

District Ranger
Livingston, MT 59047
(406) 222-7324

Helena National Forest

District Ranger
Helena, MT 59601
(406) 449-5490

Lewis and Clark National Forest

District Ranger
Choteau, MT 59422
(406) 466-5771

District Ranger
Neihart, MT 59465
(406) 236-5511

Lolo National Forest

District Ranger
Seeley Lake, MT 59858
(406) 677-2233

District Ranger
Missoula, MT 59801
(406) 329-3113

Other

Glacier National Park
West Glacier, MT 59936
(406) 888-5441

Yellowstone National Park
Yellowstone National Park, WY 82190
(307) 344-7381

Wyoming

Ski information

Jackson Hole
(307) 733-2291

Road conditions

Statewide
(307) 733-9966

Buffalo
(307) 684-9966

Casper
(307) 237-8411

Cody
(307) 587-9966

Jackson
(307) 733-9966

Lander
(307) 332-9966

Laramie
(307) 742-8981

Rawlins
(307) 324-9966

Sheridan
(307) 674-9966

Southeast Wyoming
(except Rawlins, Laramie, Cheyenne)
Toll free (800) 442-8321

Teton Park
(307) 733-2220

U.S. Forest Service

Bighorn National Forest

Buffalo Ranger District
P.O. Box 398
Buffalo, WY 82834
(307) 684-7981

Tensleep Ranger District
2009 Big Horn Avenue
Worland, WY 82401
(307) 347-8291

Tongue Ranger District
P.O. Box 2046
Sheridan, WY 82801
(307) 672-5845

Bridger-Teton National Forest

Hoback Ranger District
P.O. Box 1689
Jackson, WY 83001
(307) 733-4755

Gros Ventre Ranger District
P.O. Box 1689
Jackson, WY 83001
(307) 733-3381

Buffalo Ranger District
Blackrock Ranger Station
P.O. Box 278
Moran, WY 83013
(307) 543-2386

Pinedale Ranger District
P.O. Box 220
Pinedale, WY 82941
(307) 367-4326

Medicine Bow National Forest

Forest Supervisor's Office
605 Skyline Drive
Laramie, WY 82070
(307) 745-8971

Brush Creek Ranger District
212 South First Street
Saratoga, WY 82331
(307) 326-5258

Laramie Peak Ranger District
809 South Ninth
Douglas, WY 82633
(307) 358-4690

Shoshone National Forest

Forest Supervisor's Office
P.O. Box 2140
Cody, WY 82414
(307) 587-2274

Wapiti Ranger District
P.O. Box 2140
Cody, WY 82414
(307) 587-3291

Wind River Ranger District
P.O. Box 186
Dubois, WY 82513
(307) 455-2466

Other

Grand Teton National Park
Moose, WY 83012
(307) 733-2880

Yellowstone National Park
Yellowstone National Park, WY 82190
(307) 344-7381

Utah

Ski and snow conditions

(900) 976-9378

From Salt Lake
521-8102

Snow Report

(801) 521-8102

Road conditions

(801) 532-6000

U.S. Forest Service

Dixie National Forest

Cedar City Ranger District
P.O. Box 627
Cedar City, UT 84720
(801) 586-4462

Powell Ranger District
P.O. Box 291
Panguitch, UT 83759
(801) 676-8815

Uinta National Forest

Forest Supervisor's Office
P.O. Box 1428
Provo, UT 84601
(801) 377-5780

Heber Ranger District
P.O. Box 190
Heber City, UT 84032
(801) 654-0470

Wasatch National Forest

Forest Supervisor's Office
8226 Federal Building
125 South State Street
Salt Lake City, UT 84111
(801) 524-5030

Salt Lake Ranger District
6944 South 3000 East
Salt Lake City, UT 84109
(801) 524-5042

Kamas Ranger District
P.O. Box 68
Kamas, UT 84036
(801) 783-4338

Other

Bryce Canyon National Park
Bryce Canyon, UT 84717
(801) 834-5322

Cedar Breaks National Monument
P.O. Box 749
Cedar City, UT 84720
(801) 586-9451

Index

Absaroka-Beartooth Wilderness Area 92, 96
Albion Basin 170
All Seasons Motel 88
Alta, UT 170, 171, 173, 183
Amtrak 13, 14, 17
Anaconda, MT 58, 59, 60
Antelope Butte Ski Area 132, 133, 134, 136
Antelope Road 106
Antlers Bar 53
Arrowhead Lodge 132, 134, 135
Aspen-Mirror Lake 181
Augusta, MT 72
Autumn Creek Trail 13
Avalanche Creek Campground 16

Basin, MT 63
Bear Flat Saloon 178
Bear Lodge 132, 133, 134, 136
Bear River 156
Beartooth-Absaroka Wilderness 89
Beartooth Pass 89
Beaver, UT 174
Beaverhead Range 55
Beaverhead XC Ski Club 54
Belton Station 13, 17
Berry Meadows Road 62
Big Cottonwood Canyon 166, 167, 169, 171
Big Hole Basin 53
Big Hole Battlefield 53
Big Horn Mountain Shop 134
Big Horn Mountains 133, 136, 139, 140
Big Mountain 20
Big Sky, MT 78
Big Sky Ski Area 79, 80
Big Timber, MT 90, 94, 97
Bigfork, MT 29, 31
Bill Koch Youth Ski League 44
Billings, MT 94
Bitterroot Range 35, 44
Bitterroot Valley 39, 47
Black Mountain Lookout 136
Blind Miner Restaurant 169
Blue Spruce Cafe 132, 133, 134, 136
Bob Marshall Wilderness 27, 72
Boulder, MT 62, 63, 64, 66
Boulder Hot Springs 62, 65, 66, 67
Bozeman, MT 78, 82, 124
Bradley Lake 104, 106
Brian Head, UT 176, 178, 182, 184
Brian Head Nordic Ski Shop 176, 177, 178, 182
Brian Head Peak 177
Brian Head Ski Area 177
Bridger, MT 139
Bridger Bowl Ski Area 82
Bridger Canyon 84
Bridger Mountain Lodge 82
Bridger-Teton National Forest 112, 113, 114
Bridger Wilderness 115
Brighton, UT 166, 169, 170, 171
Brighton Ski Touring Center 166, 167, 169
Bristlecone Hostel 176, 177
Brothers Cafe 21
Brown Derby 60
Bryce Canyon 177, 182, 184, 185, 186, 187
Bryce Canyon Lodge 187
Bryce Point 185, 186
Buffalo, WY 138
Buffalo Bill Historical, Center 122
Burgess Junction, WY 132
Burlington Northern Railway 11
Burnt Leather Ranch 90, 91
Butte, MT 54, 58, 59, 66

Cabin Fever Days 16, 21
Cache Creek Trail 110
Camp Creek 47
Camp Creek Inn 112, 113
Casper, WY 139, 142, 143, 144
Casper Mountain 143
Cedar Breaks National Monument 176, 177, 182

Cedar City, UT 174, 180, 183, 184
Centennial, WY 150
Charles Russell Gallery 73
Chateau Apres Lodge 154, 155, 162
Chico Hot Springs 86, 87
Choteau, MT 70
Cliff Creek Trail 113
Cloud Peak Wilderness Area 133, 138
Cody, WY 118, 119, 120, 122

Cold Creek 28
Cold Lake 28
Colter Pass 89
Comet, MT 65
Comet Mountain 55
Condon, MT 26, 30
Continental Divide 13, 47, 129
Cooke City, MT 86, 88, 89, 96, 122
Coolidge City, MT 55
Cora, WY 115
Coram, MT 14
Cornice Crashers Ski Tours 180, 182
Cottonwood Creek 106
Cow Track Restaurant 73
Crazy Mountain Sports 86
Crystal Lakes Resort 22, 23

DJ's Sports 142
Daniels Canyon 162
Darby, MT 38, 42
Dayton, WY 134
Dead Indian Summit 119
Deer Haven Lodge 138, 140
Deerlodge National Forest 59, 60
Dentons Point 60
Desert Mountain 15
Desert Mountain Guest Ranch 14, 15
Dew Drop Inn 16
Dillon, MT 50, 54
Discovery Basin Ski Area 58
Ditch Creek 104, 106
Divide Road 74, 76
Douglas, WY 142, 143
Dubois, WY 128, 131
Duck Creek Village 180, 183

Eagles Nest Lodge 95, 96, 97
Ear Mountain 73
East Glacier, MT 10
Echo Lake Road 29
Elkhorn Hot Springs 54, 55
Elkhorn Mine 55
Elkhorn Range 66, 68
Elkhorn Saloon 88
Emigrant, MT 87
Emigrant Gulch 88
Emigrant Peak 88
Encampment, WY 146
Essex, MT 10, 13
Esterbrook Lodge 142, 143
Evanston, WY 143, 156

Fairmont Hot Springs 58, 59
Fairy Falls 127
Fairyland View 185, 186
Ferdinand's 178
Fetty's 53
Fish Creek 47
Flagg Ranch 100, 101, 110
Flaming Arrow Ski Touring Centre 82, 83
Flathead Lake 31
Flathead National Forest 10, 13
Fortine, MT 22
French Creek Campground 150
Friendly Store and Motel 150
Ft. Benton, MT 76, 77

Galena Gulch 63, 65
Galena Park 65
Gallatin Range 55
Gardiner, MT 86
Georgetown Lake 58, 59, 60
Glacier Highland 17
Glacier National Park 10, 13, 15, 16
Glendo, WY 142
Going to the Sun Highway 16
Grand Teton National Park 101, 102, 104, 108, 109
Granite Hot Springs 113
Granite Pass 133
Grasshopper Valley 55
Grassy Lake Road 101
Great Falls, MT 10, 70, 73, 74, 76
Great Northern Railway 11
Gregson Hot Springs 59
Greybull, WY 132, 134
Guest Ranch Road 26

Hamilton, MT 38, 42, 46
Hawley Mountain Guest Ranch 94, 95
Heber, UT 158, 162
Heidelburg Inn 107
Helena, MT 62, 66, 77
High Mountain Helicopter Skiing 110
High Uinta Primitive Area 156
Hoback Junction, WY 112
Holland Lake 31
Holland Lake Lodge 30, 31

Holland Peak 32
Homestead 162,163
Hoosiers' Motel 88
Hotel Wolf 144, 145
Hoyt Canyon 161
Huckleberry Hot Springs 101
Hungry Horse, MT 14
Hungry Hunky 21

Idaho Falls, ID 124
Independence, MT 96
Inspiration Point 185
Irma Hotel 122
Irma Mine 89
Izaak Walton Inn 10, 11
Jackson, MT 50, 51, 53
Jackson, WY 100, 104, 108, 112, 114
Jackson Creek 53
Jackson Hole 104, 107, 109
Jackson Hole Ski Tours 110
Jackson Hot Springs 50, 51
Jedediah's Sourdough 111
Jefferson Creek 74, 76
Jenny Lake 104, 106
Jewell Basin 29
Jones Creek Trail 72
Kalispell, MT 10, 14, 26, 29
Kamas, UT 158
Kelly, WY 110
King's Hill 74, 76

Lake McDonald 16
Lame Duck Restaurant 111
Land of 10,000 Haystacks 53
Lander, WY 128
Laramie, WY 150
Laramie Mountains 143
Las Vegas, NV 176
Lewis and Clark National Forest 70, 76
Lindbergh Lake 32
Little Belt Mountains 76
Little Cottonwood Canyon 170, 173
Little Milk Creek 53
Livingston, MT 86, 90, 92, 94
Lolo, MT 34
Lolo Hot Springs 34, 35
Lolo Pass 34, 36
Lone Mountain Ranch 78, 79
Lost Horse Nordic Village 40, 42, 43
Lost Trail Hot Springs Resort 46, 47
Lost Trail Ski Area 46, 48
Lowell, WY 132, 134

Ma Perkins Cafe 88
Main Boulder Road 94
Mammoth Hot Springs 86, 88
Marion, UT 158
Martin City, MT 16
Marysvale, UT 187
Maverick Mountain Ski Area 55
McLeod, MT 90, 94
Meadeau View Lodge 180, 181, 184
Meadowlark Lake 139
Meadowlark Resort 138, 139
Meadowlark Ski Area 138
Meagher County Poor Farm 75
Medicine Bow Lodge 144, 147, 148, 149
Medicine Bow National Forest 143, 144
Medicine Bow Ski Area 150
Midway, UT 162
Milford, UT 175
Mill Creek 88
Million Dollar Cowboy Club 110
Mineral Springs Hotel 34, 35
Mission Camp 92
Mission Mountains 27, 31
Missoula, MT 26, 29, 30, 34, 38, 46, 48
Missouri River 77
Mister P's 21
Molly Green's Pub 169
Monarch, MT 74, 76
Montana Sports Ranch 26, 27
Montana State Sled Dog Championships 43
Montana State University 84, 96
Moran, WY 100, 107
Moose, WY 104, 106, 107
Moose Creek Trail 47
Moran, WY 100, 107
Morning Glory Pool 125, 127
Mt. Hawley 96
Mt. Holly Ski Resort 174, 175
Mt. Lockhart 72
Mt. Majestic Manor 169
Mt. Timpanogos 161
Mus' Rest Motel 88

Neihart, MT 76, 77
North Absaroka Wilderness 120, 122

Oakley, UT 158
Old Faithful 102, 125, 126
Old Faithful Snow Lodge 102, 124, 125
Old North Trail 73
Old Saloon 89
Opportunity, MT 58
Owl's Nest Restaurant 135
Oxbow Bend 104, 106

Pahaska Tepee 120, 121
Panguitch, UT 187
Panguitch Lake 176
Paradise Valley 87
Paria Valley 186
Paria View 185
Park City, UT 154, 155, 156, 157, 158, 162, 164, 170, 171
Parowan, UT 175, 176
Paulsin Basin 161
Perkins Restaurant 133
Peterson's Corral 58, 59
Philipsburg, MT 58, 60
Pinedale, WY 114, 116
Pintlar Mountains 59, 60
Piute Creek Outfitters 158, 159, 164
Polar Bar 56
Polaris, MT 54, 56
Polaris Mine 56
Poor Farm 74, 75
Powder River Pass 140
Powderhound Nordic 110
Pray, MT 86
Provo, UT 162
Provo Canyon 161
Puffer Lake 174

Radon Mine 65
Rawhide Ranch 118, 119
Rawlins, WY 144, 149
Red Butte 28
Red Lodge, MT 89, 122
Rendezvous Ski Shop 124
Republic Mountain 89
Rock Springs, WY 114
Roosville, B.C. 22
Rose's Cantina 51, 53
Ross' Hole 47
Round Meadow 20
Ruby's Inn 184, 185
Salmon, ID 46, 47
Salt Lake City, UT 129, 154, 157, 158, 162, 166, 167, 170, 173
Salt Lake Valley 167
Saratoga, WY 144, 146, 148, 149, 150
Seeley Lake 30, 32
7 Lazy P Guest Ranch 70, 71
Sheridan, WY 132, 133, 134

Shoofly 89
Shoshone National Forest 119, 120, 129
Shoshone River 122
Showdown Ski Area 76
Sibley Lake 136
Silver Dollar Bar 111
Silver Fork 168
Silver Fork Lodge 166, 167
Sisson Hotel 145
Skinny Skis Ski Shop 104, 110
Skyline Drive 114
Sleeping Child Hot Springs Resort 38, 39
Smith Creek 29
Snake River 101, 106
Snow Goose Nordic Shop 42
Snow King Ski Area 110
Snowmobile Capital of the World 127
Snowpine Lodge 170, 171
Snowy Range 144, 147
Snowy Range Pass 150
Solarium Point 55
South French Creek Road 150
South Mountain 161
Spa Motel 77
Spanish Peaks Wilderness Area 80
Star Meadows Ranch 18, 19
Strawberry Reservoir 162
Sula, MT 46
Sunlight Basin 119
Sunlight Basin Road 118, 119
Sunlight Trail 122
Sunset Point 185, 186
Sunshine Health Mines 62, 63
Swan Lake 32
Swan Range 31
Swan River Valley 31

Taggart Lake 104, 106
Ten Lakes Scenic Area 22
Ten Sleep, WY 138, 139, 140
Teton Canyon 70, 71, 72
Teton Hot Pots 111
Teton Mountain Touring 110
Teton Mountains 105, 107
Teton Pass (MT) 70
Teton Pass (WY) 107
Teton Pass Ski Area 72
Teton River 72
Teton Science School 106
Teton Village Ski Area 110
The Old Corral 150
Thunder Inn 183
Togwotee Pass 128, 129
Townsend, MT 43
Triangle X Ranch 104, 105, 110
Two Bear Trail 40

Uinta Mountains 156, 161
Uinta National Forest 154

Village Store 169

Walcott Junction, WY 146
Waldron Creek 72
Warm Springs Creek 53
Wasatch Formation 186
Wasatch Mountain State Park 163
Wasatch Mountains 155, 161, 163, 167, 171
Wasatch National Forest 167
Waugh Gulch 48
West Boulder Road 90
West Camp Creek Campground 48
West Glacier, MT 10, 13, 14, 15, 17
West Yellowstone, MT 78, 102, 124, 127
Western Motel 108, 109
White City 88
White Pine Lodge 114, 115
White Pine Touring Center 154, 155, 162
White Stallion Trail 40
White Sulphur Springs, MT 74, 76, 77
Whitefish, MT 14, 18, 20, 22, 29, 30
Willow Park Picnic Ground 138, 139, 140
Wilson, WY 107
Wind River Mountains 115, 116, 129
Wind River Ranch Ski Lodge 128, 129
Wisdom, MT 50, 53
Woody Creek 53
Worland, WY 138
Wort Hotel 111

Yellowstone National Park 78, 80, 86, 94, 96, 100, 101, 102, 104, 120, 123, 128
Yellowstone Nordic Wilderness Shop 124

Zion Overlook 181
Zion Park 182

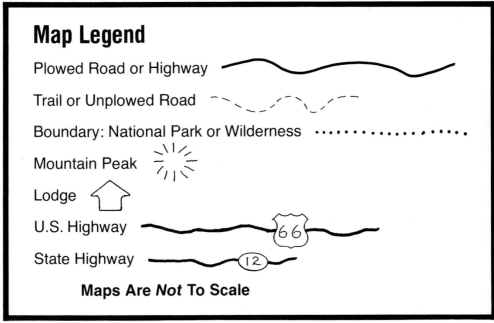

Map Legend

Plowed Road or Highway

Trail or Unplowed Road

Boundary: National Park or Wilderness

Mountain Peak

Lodge

U.S. Highway

State Highway

Maps Are *Not* To Scale

Notes

Recreational area winter parking permits are not mandated in the three states, Montana, Wyoming and Utah. Motorists are required, however, to abide by local traffic regulations and directional signs.

Studded tires are permitted as follows: Montana — metal studs may be used October 1 through May 31; Utah — state-approved *soft* studs are legal October 15 through March 31; Wyoming has no restrictions.

Privately-owned facilities established on national forest land operate under special use permits authorized and issued by the U.S. Forest Service.

All temperatures noted herein are reported in Fahrenheit.

Lodging rates and other prices were current at the time of publication.